The Church That
Will Be
LEFT BEHIND

by R. L. Hymers, Jr.
M.Div., D.Min., Th.D.

With a foreword by
Dr. James O. Combs,
Associate Editor of the
TIM LA HAYE PROPHECY
STUDY BIBLE

ABOUT THE AUTHOR

R. L. Hymers, Jr. is a graduate of the California State University at Los Angeles (B.A.), Golden Gate Baptist Theological Seminary, Southern Baptist (M.Div.), San Francisco Theological Seminary, United Presbyterian (D.Min.) and Louisiana Baptist Theological Seminary, Baptist Bible Fellowship (Th.D.). He and his wife, Ileana, are the parents of twin sons, Robert Leslie III and John Wesley. Dr. Hymers worked with Southern Baptist churches for many years. He became a fundamentalist by reading the books and sermons of the late Dr. John R. Rice. Dr. Hymers is the founding pastor of the Fundamentalist Baptist Tabernacle, the only Baptist church in the civic center of Los Angeles. Known for his strong stand for Biblical inerrancy and inner-city evangelism, Dr. Hymers is an unashamed old-time fundamentalist, who earnestly contends for the faith in the tradition of J. Frank Norris, John R. Rice, Bob Jones, Sr., and "Fighting Bob" Shuler. He has been in the ministry over forty-three years.

+ +

ADDRESS AND WEBSITE

You can write to Dr. Hymers for a list of his books and tapes at

P. O. Box 15308
Los Angeles, CA 90015.

His website is at

www.rlhymersjr.com.

DISCLAIMER

The people or sources mentioned in this book do not necessarily carry the endorsement of Dr. Hymers or the Fundamentalist Baptist Tabernacle of Los Angeles.

+ +

Printed in the United States of America.

Published by:
Hearthstone Publishing, Ltd.
P. O. Box 815, Oklahoma City, OK 73101
405/789-3885   888/891-3300   FAX 405/789-6502

ISBN 1-57558-083-7

PREFACE

by

the author

This book was written particularly for the layman, although I think preachers will find it interesting and helpful. It is not meant to be a comprehensive study of Bible prophecy. The book presents several themes related to prophecy, with an evangelistic aim throughout. It is meant to help those who have an interest in Bible prophecy but have not yet been truly regenerated. I hope it meets that need for many, and that they will experience real conversion while reading it. I also hope that it will encourage true Christians, and especially pastors, to be more zealous in winning the lost in the closing days of this dispensation.

I wish to thank my colleague, Dr. Christopher Cagan, for valuable advice and for typing the manuscript. Without him this book could not have been written. I also wish to thank Dr. Noah Hutchings for suggesting the title and Hearthstone Publishing, Ltd. for putting this book into print. Special thanks go to Dr. James O. Combs for offering extensive help and for writing the foreword, and to the editors of the *Tim LaHaye Prophecy Study Bible* for valuable insights, gleaned from their study notes.

May this little book be used by God to "turn many to righteousness as the stars forever and ever" (Daniel 12:3).

Dr. R. L. Hymers, Jr.
The Pastor's Study
March 25, 2001

This book is dedicated to
Ileana, my helper and my wife,
and to my fine sons,
Robert Leslie III and John Wesley.
I thank God for all three of them every day.

TABLE OF CONTENTS

FOREWORD

by

Dr. James O. Combs

Provost of Louisiana Baptist University and Theological Seminary,
former editor of the *Baptist Bible Tribune,*
Associate editor of the *Tim LaHaye Prophecy Study Bible*

This is a much needed book, which will challenge you to "Examine yourselves, whether ye be in the faith" (II Corinthians 13:5).

When the rapture occurs all true Christians will be "caught up... in the clouds, to meet the Lord in the air" (I Thessalonians 4:17). On the other hand, all unsaved preachers and religious but lost lay people will be left behind. In this insightful book Dr. Hymers examines the plight and destiny of those who are left on earth.

This book can be a powerful evangelistic tool even before the rapture, to cause lost church members to reevaluate their spiritual condition and make their calling and election sure (II Peter 1:10).

This book may also be used to lead many to Christ after the rapture. Even in judgment, God has mercy, as Dr. Hymers shows.

II Thessalonians 2:3-4 seems to indicate that those "left behind" will be prime prospects as followers of the Man of Sin, the coming Antichrist.

Now is the time to heed the warnings in this book lest you, curious reader, be *left behind.*

May God use this book to awaken lost sinners who are part of the visible church, that some might be saved.

CHAPTER ONE

A WARNING TO THOSE WHO
THINK THEY ARE SAVED

"Then shall two be in the field; the one shall be taken,
and the other left. Two women shall be grinding at the
mill; the one shall be taken, and the other left"
(Matthew 24:40-41).

I am convinced that many people who think they are saved are
actually lost. I believe that they will be left behind when Jesus
comes. The "rapture" refers to the time when Jesus returns and true
Christians will suddenly be caught up to meet Him in the air (cf. I
Corinthians 15:52-54; I Thessalonians 4:14-18).

The thought of being lifted up to Heaven gives us wonderful
hope. But many who expect to be raptured will be left behind to face
the horrors that will then come on earth. The Bible tells us that great
judgment and agony will be experienced by those who are left
behind:

"Woe to the inhabiters of the earth and of the sea! For
the devil is come down unto you, having great wrath,
because he knoweth that he hath but a short time"
(Revelation 12:12).

Thousands who think they are saved will not be prepared. They
will not be raptured. They will be left on the earth to be tormented
by the Devil in a series of dreadful persecutions.

You Know Not When the Master Will Come

Jesus gave a great parable, a truth-filled illustration, to warn you
not to miss the rapture:

"For the Son of man is as a man taking a far journey,
who left his house, and gave authority to his servants,

1

and to every man his work, and commanded the porter to watch. Watch ye therefore: for ye know not when the master of the house cometh, at even, or at midnight, or at the cockcrowing, or in the morning: Lest coming suddenly he find you sleeping. And what I say unto you I say unto all, Watch" (Mark 13:34-37).

Dr. James O. Combs, former editor of the **Baptist Bible Tribune**, and associate editor of the **Tim LaHaye Prophecy Study Bible**, tells us that this passage of Scripture refers to the rapture:

> The parable found only in Mark 13:23-37...can refer only to the commanded expectant attitude of all New Testament believers from the first century until now, who are urged to "watch ye therefore: for ye know not when the Master of the House (Jesus) cometh, at even, or at midnight, or at the cockcrowing, of in the morning, lest coming suddenly He find you sleeping..." This is relevant to Gentile believers as well as Jewish believers, since Mark wrote particularly to Romans, who would know little of Jewish thought (James O. Combs, **Some Observations About the Return of Christ in the Olivet Discourse**, privately published, pp. 1-2).

Dr. Combs says that the rapture could come at any time, and Christ gave us a warning in this passage. If you are "sleeping" you will be **left behind!** "Lest coming suddenly he find you sleeping" (Mark 13:36). A person who is "sleeping" is religious but lost. Such a person is not truly converted and will not be raptured when Jesus comes. A person like this will be left on earth. You may be in this situation yourself. You ought to think about that very seriously.

Dr. James Binney is the director of Moorehead Manor and the editor of **Issues of the Heart Journal.** In an article titled, "Can Church Members Go to Hell?", Dr. Binney said:

> When I first became a Christian, I assumed that all church going people were automatically qualified for the fast track into heaven. It was a given. After becoming a church member, then a pastor, I had to rethink the issue.

> I have encountered many leaders who doubted their
> faith, others who could not clearly explain how they
> were saved, and even others who frankly admitted that
> they had never been saved. Imagine 20 pastors
> confessing their lost condition in one city! It
> happened…when George Whitefield preached in
> Boston. Dr. Bob Jones, Sr. said, "I have spent nearly
> my entire life in association with ministers. Nobody
> would tell you that every preacher in America is a
> saved man." (Jim Binney, *Issues of the Heart*, Fall
> 2000, p. 2).

Dr. Binney believes that many ministers are lost today. These
preachers will be unprepared when the rapture comes!

Dr. Binney also believes that many church members are
unsaved. He refers to several well-known Christian leaders to
support his position:

> Dr. Rod Bell, president of the Fundamental Baptist
> Fellowship of America, estimates that 50% of church
> people are without Christ. His estimate concurs with
> that of Bob Jones, Sr. …in the 1940's he also fixed the
> estimate at 50%. Dr. B. R. Lakin estimated that 75%
> are lost. W. A. Criswell would be surprised to see even
> 25% of his church members in heaven. Dr. Bob Gray,
> longtime pastor of the prestigious Trinity Baptist
> Church of Jacksonville, Florida, once said that
> probably 75% of those he baptized were not saved.
> Billy Graham put the figure at 85% (several years ago)
> while A. W. Tozer and Southern Baptist consultant Jim
> Elliff raise it to 90%. These are shocking figures to be
> sure, but not surprising…many such lost people find
> their way into the roles of the church through
> evangelism methods that are less than thorough…In a
> country boasting of coast to coast Christianity with
> thousands of church buildings and millions of
> members, it is hard to realize the depth of the
> problem…The reason that so many who think they are
> saved may actually be lost is traceable to a
> misunderstanding about the means of salvation. *Many*

religious people are misled into believing they are genuine Christians because of some external criteria. This may be the form of their prayer at the time of salvation. *It can also include a dependence upon feelings, going forward at a public meeting, or meeting someone's expectations in any regard about the means of salvation.* The Bible warns against dependency upon the wrong things for salvation (Jim Binney, *Issues of the Heart*, Fall 2000, p. 4).

I have quoted this nationally-known Bible teacher and counselor at length because he has made the problem so very clear. When a leading evangelical like Dr. A. W. Tozer said that 90% of the members of our churches were lost we are in trouble! Even Billy Graham once said that 85% of our church members were unsaved! These are frightening estimates. If they come anywhere near being correct, *you* may be in trouble.

The End of This Age

Jesus gave us this warning:

> "But as the days of Noe (Noah) were, so shall also the coming of the Son of man be...(they) knew not until the flood came, and took them all away; so shall also the coming of the Son of man be. Then shall two be in the field; the one shall be taken, and the other left. Two women shall be grinding at the mill; the one shall be taken, and the other left" (Matthew 24:37-41).

Dr. James O. Combs comments on those verses:

> Some being taken and others left is a description of the translation (the rapture) of the living saints (Christians); the admonitions to "watch" in the adjoining verses are relevant to the believers at the close of the Church Age, prior to the Rapture (James O. Combs, *Some Observations About the Return of Christ in the Olivet Discourse*, p. 3).

4

Dr. David L. Cooper was a teacher and mentor of Tim LaHaye, the co-author of the best-selling *Left Behind* books. Dr. Cooper said this concerning Matthew 24:37-42, the "one taken and the other left" passage:

> At the time of which Jesus is speaking, men and women will be eating and drinking, marrying and giving in marriage, buying and selling. Various passages of Scripture show that such will not be the condition of the world and of the human family at the very end of the Tribulation, because the devastating, thoroughgoing judgments will wreck the physical earth, as well as civilization. Since in Matthew 24:32-44, Jesus says that at His coming mankind will be following the normal pursuits of life, He must be referring to His coming for His saints before the Tribulation; in other words, at the time of the rapture (David L. Cooper, quoted in *Some Observations About the Return of Christ in the Olivet Discourse* by James O. Combs, p. 3).

This is a warning to *you!*

> "Then shall two be in the field; the one shall be taken, and the other left. Two women shall be grinding at the mill; the one shall be taken, and the other left" (Matthew 24:40-41).

As Larry Norman put it,

> Man and wife asleep in bed,
> She hears a noise and turns her head – he's gone.
> I wish we'd all been ready.
> Two men walking up a hill,
> One disappears and one's left standing still,
> I wish we'd all been ready.
>
> There's no time to change your mind,
> How could you have been so blind?
> The Father spoke, the demons dined,
> The Son has come, and you've been left behind,
> You've been left behind, you've been left behind.
>   ("I Wish We'd All Been Ready" by Larry Norman, 1969).

The "Left Behind" Novels

The *Left Behind* novels by Tim LaHaye and Jerry B. Jenkins are the fastest selling Christian books ever published. Beginning with the rapture of true Christians, as related in the Bible, LaHaye and Jenkins portray the tribulations that will be experienced on earth by those who are not raptured.

The *Left Behind* series has sold in the millions. These books give the events that follow the rapture in the form of eight novels, with more to come. The authors follow the basic view, given in the Bible, of the Tribulation period, the dark seven-year epoch that will come when the Antichrist is the final world dictator. I find little fault with the series. The books are written as Christian fiction, so the authors of necessity fill in details that are not actually in the Scriptures. But the basic events are firmly grounded in the Bible.

My main objection to these books is that I think far too many people are portrayed as being raptured. If the figures of true converts given by W. A. Criswell, Bob Jones, Sr., A. W. Tozer and others are anywhere close to being accurate, the majority of those who think they are saved will not be raptured. The chaos created by the disappearance of millions of people, as portrayed in the *Left Behind* series, will not happen – if the leading Christians we have quoted are correct in their estimates of how few are truly converted.

Evangelist Luis Palau is one of the most well known evangelical leaders of our time. Not long ago, Palau said:

> America, where 80 percent of the people claim to be Christians, but few live any differently from pagans or atheists, as though God has no claim on their lives. *Their hearts have not been changed* (Luis Palau, *The Only Hope for America*, Crossway Books, 1996, p. 10).

Dr. James Dobson, of Focus on the Family, said:

> Many laymen do not know that the institution of the church is undergoing serious difficulty at this time. Many local churches are barely surviving with approximately 3,000-4,000 of them closing their doors

6

every year. Pollster George Barna compares the church to the "Titanic." He said, "It is large, elegant, and sinking fast." Attendance at weekly religious activities in the United States has continued to slip from 49 percent in 1991 to 37 percent today. Furthermore, 80 percent of church growth results from transfer of memberships. These statistics tell us that evangelism is largely stagnant. Something is wrong with this picture. ***Obviously, the majority of Americans are dabbling in religious expression that has no substance*** (James Dobson, Focus on the Family newsletter, August, 1998, p. 2).

Palau and Dobson are aware of the fact that many church members are lost. And they are not alone by any means. The great British preacher and author Dr. Martyn Lloyd-Jones spoke of "the terrible apostasy that has increasingly characterized the church for the last hundred years" (Martyn Lloyd-Jones, ***Revival***, Crossway Books, 1987, p. 57). Dr. Lloyd-Jones is correct when he indicates that we are now in a dark period of apostasy. That's why I think many who claim to be "born again" Christians will be left on earth at the rapture.

After hearing countless testimonies, it is my opinion that a very large number of those who attend our churches every Sunday are actually lost people, including Sunday School teachers, deacons, pastor's wives, and even pastors themselves.

The late Dr. Monroe "Monk" Parker was often called "The Dean of American Evangelists." Dr. Parker once said:

If we could get half the church members saved, we would have a mighty revival. In fact, I think, if we could get half of the preachers in America converted, we would see a mighty revival (Monroe Parker, ***Through Sunshine and Shadows: My First Seventy-Seven Years***, Sword of the Lord, 1987, pp. 61-62).

If this aged and honored evangelist was close to being right, think how many will be left behind at the rapture.

How about you? Will you be left behind? The purpose of this book is to make you think about that dreadful possibility.

The Wise and Foolish Virgins

In Matthew 25:1-13 Jesus gave the parable of the Wise and Foolish Virgins:

> "Then shall the kingdom of heaven be likened unto ten
> virgins, which took their lamps, and went forth to meet
> the bridegroom. And five of them were wise, and five
> were foolish. They that were foolish took their lamps,
> and took no oil with them: But the wise took oil in their
> vessels with their lamps. While the bridegroom tarried,
> they all slumbered and slept. And at midnight there was
> a cry made, Behold, the bridegroom cometh; go ye out
> to meet him. Then all those virgins arose, and trimmed
> their lamps. And the foolish said unto the wise, Give us
> of your oil; for our lamps are gone out. But the wise
> answered, saying, Not so; lest there be not enough for
> us and you: but go ye rather to them that sell, and buy
> for yourselves. And while they went to buy, the
> bridegroom came; and they that were ready went in
> with him to the marriage: and the door was shut.
> Afterward came also the other virgins, saying, Lord,
> Lord, open to us. But he answered and said, Verily I
> say unto you, I know you not. Watch therefore, for ye
> know neither the day nor the hour wherein the Son of
> man cometh" (Matthew 25:1-13).

Dr. James O. Combs comments:

> The parable of the Wise and Foolish Virgins *refers to
> the Church Age*, to Christians at the close of this age,
> and therefore is a parabolic description of the Rapture.
> This is why we are commanded to "watch" (James O.
> Combs, *Some Observations About the Return of
> Christ in the Olivet Discourse*, p. 1).

Dr. Arno C. Gaebelein, consulting editor of the *Scofield Study Bible*, was in agreement with Dr. Combs' position. He said this concerning the parable of the Wise and Foolish Virgins:

> The parable of the virgins describes Christendom and what will take place some day...the midnight cry aroused entire Christendom again...and still the cry is heard till He comes (Arno C. Gaebelein, note in the *Annotated Bible*, the Gospel of Matthew, p. 52).

Dr. Wilbur M. Smith was also in full agreement with Dr. Combs and Dr. Gaebelein regarding the parable of the Wise and Foolish Virgins. Dr. Smith was a respected professor at the Moody Bible Institute for many years. He said:

> I believe that Dr. Gaebelein is correct in his comment on these verses (Matthew 25:1-13): "It is noteworthy that the condition is stated first, the demonstration of it comes later: after the midnight cry had been sounded the foolishness of the five becomes manifested. The division of the virgins in five wise and five foolish brings out the fact that in the professing church two classes of people are found, the true and false, saved and unsaved, professing and possessing. The wise represent such who have believed in the Lord Jesus Christ, who have a personal knowledge of Christ and are sealed with the Spirit (i.e. they are converted); they have the unction of the Holy One, who is represented by the oil. The foolish are such who have the form of godliness and deny the power thereof. ***They represent such who have taken the outward profession (of salvation) but lack the reality.*** As they have never truly trusted in Christ they have no oil, the Holy Spirit. The objection has been made that the foolish virgins can hardly represent unsaved persons, because they are called virgins and went out to meet the Bridegroom. In their profession they were virgins, and in profession they had gone out to meet the Bridegroom (Christ). Another objection is raised. Did they not later say, "Give us of your oil, for our lamps have gone out?" Then they must have had some oil, else how could they say their lamps were gone out? There is no proof at all in this that they had a certain supply of oil. It is distinctly said that they only took lamps, but they did not take oil. They may have made an attempt to light the wicks of their lamps only to see that they did not

give light and went out." – A. C. Gaebelein (comments
by Wilbur M. Smith and Arno C. Gaebelein in
Peloubet's Notes, 1948).

Dr. Combs, Dr. Gaebelein, and Dr. Wilbur M. Smith all agree that the
parable refers to Christians at the rapture. They teach that Matthew
25:10 refers to the rapture itself:

> "And while they went to buy, the bridegroom came; and
> they that were ready went in with him (Christ) to the
> marriage: and the door was shut" (Matthew 25:10).

This is the basic view of Bible teacher Dave Hunt as well.
Combs, Gaebelein, Wilbur Smith, and Mr. Hunt believe that Matthew
25:10 refers to the rapture, and *I am convinced that they are right.*
For hundreds of years leading preachers such as George Whitefield,
Gilbert Tennent, Asahel Nettleton, Duncan Campbell, and a host of
others, including Spurgeon, preached Matthew 25:1-13 as a warning
to church members, telling them that they might not be ready for the
coming of Christ. Some of these old-time preachers may have been
off on other points of prophecy, but they were basically right in
preaching this parable as a warning to the lost. The passage ends
with these stark words,

> "And the door was shut. Afterward came also the other
> virgins, saying, Lord, Lord, open to us. But he
> answered and said, Verily I say unto you, I know you
> not. Watch therefore, for ye know neither the day nor
> the hour wherein the Son of man cometh" (Matthew
> 25:10-13).

When the rapture comes, many who think they are saved will be
disappointed. They will find they had false conversions and are not
ready to "go in with him to the marriage" (Matthew 25:10) – "and the
door was shut."

My associate, Dr. Christopher Cagan, heard about the rapture
one evening before he became a Christian. As a Jew he rejected it.
But late that night he had a dream that the true Christians were caught
away and he was left. This was one of the things that led to his
conversion.

10

Do you want to take a chance on being shut out of Heaven when the rapture comes? Do you want to gamble with your soul and reject the teachings of Combs, Gaebelein, Wilbur Smith, Dave Hunt, and the plain meaning of the words themselves, "And the door was shut"? Do you want to risk the possibility of missing the rapture and being *left behind?* I believe that millions who claim to be saved will indeed be shut out at the rapture. Will you be one of them?

> Life was filled with guns and war,
> And everyone got trampled on the floor.
> I wish we'd all been ready.
> Children died, the days grew cold,
> A piece of bread could buy a bag of gold.
> I wish we'd all been ready.
>
> There's no time to change your mind,
> How could you have been so blind?
> The Father spoke, the demons dined,
> The Son has come, and you've been left behind.
> ("I Wish We'd All Been Ready" by Larry Norman, 1969).

You must turn from your sinful life-style and trust wholeheartedly in Jesus Christ, the Son of God. His Blood, shed on the Cross, will then cleanse you from sin. The living Christ, at the right hand of God in Heaven, will forgive you and save you. A truly saved person will then want to become an active member of a Bible-believing church. Only those who experience full conversion will be ready for the rapture.

> "Then shall two be in the field; the one shall be taken, and the other left. Two women shall be grinding at the mill; the one shall be taken, and the other left" (Matthew 24:40-41).

CHAPTER TWO

SIGNS OF THE LAST DAYS

"What shall be the sign of thy coming, and of the end of
the world?" (Matthew 24:3)

The disciples of Christ wanted to know when the world would
end. He gave them many signs, recorded in Matthew 24, and in the
parallel passage, in Luke 21. Matthew 24 gives many of the signs,
and Luke 21 gives the rest of them.

First, There Are Ecological Signs

Jesus predicted

> "great earthquakes...in divers places, and famines and
> pestilences; and fearful sights...and upon the earth
> distress of nations, with perplexity; the sea and the
> waves roaring; men's hearts failing them for fear, and
> for looking after those things which are coming on the
> earth" (Luke 21:11, 25-26).

Think of it! Jesus said that people's hearts would faint and fail when
they see what's happening "on the earth." He said there would be
distress and dismay and anguish and great fear because of what they
see happening on earth.

Did you read this newspaper story a short time ago? Scientists
found a hole in the ice at the North Pole as large as the State of
Maine. *Time* magazine had a news report – featured on the cover –
"The Big Meltdown. As the temperature rises in the Arctic, it sends a
chill around the planet." (*Time* magazine, September 4, 2000, pp.
52-56). The article said, "Even a partial melting could devastate the
northern hemisphere's climate."

Many scientists fear that we may be entering a new ice age. In
the *Time* article, Dr. Richard Alley, a geophysicist at Penn State
University, spoke of "dropping temperatures far (greater) than the

changes that have affected humans in recorded history." Would this
be the end of mankind? Dr. Alley says, "No, but it will be an
uncomfortable time for humanity. *Very* uncomfortable."

Scientists like Dr. Alley are literally filled *with fear* "and for
looking after those things which are coming on the earth" (Luke
21:26).

When you look at the meltdown of the North Pole and a possible
ice-age, which scientists now say could come abruptly in the next 25
to 50 years – it is frightening. When you realize that the AIDS
epidemic is devastating Africa, with no end in sight – it is
frightening. When you look at the resurgence of antibiotic resistant
tuberculosis and other new "monster" diseases that don't respond to
any known drugs – it is frightening.

No wonder so many people worry about the future. A recent
poll shows that 80 percent of today's teenagers do not think they have
a good future. It shows, particularly, that these young people often
worry about problems in ecology, like the meltdown of the North
Pole and the ice age or "waterworld" it could produce.

People I talk to seem to know instinctively that things are getting
worse. And it frightens them. What are they going to do when it's
freezing cold all year in California?

> "Men's hearts failing them for fear, and for looking after
> those things which are coming on the earth" (Luke
> 21:26).

Ralph Nader took about 3 percent of Al Gore's votes in Florida,
thus ensuring the election of Bush. Those who supported Nader are
deeply concerned that mankind is ruining our planet. And I share that
concern – completely! Enough people were thinking about
ecological problems to change the outcome of a presidential election!

My wife and I stood in our yard the other day. I asked her,
"When was the last time you saw a monarch butterfly? When was
the last time you saw a toad or a frog? They're gone – or very nearly
so." She said to me, "Yes, we've really messed up the environment."
A man at my gym said to me, "We've fouled our nest and we're
ruining the world." Sadly, I had to agree. He was *dead* right.

And the alarming ecological problems that are reported every
day in the newspapers are signs that the end of the world and the

Second Coming of Christ may be very near. *You probably don't have much time left to prepare!*

That's why you need to get into a Bible-believing church and find Christ *now!* Time is running out for our world. You ought to be in a great hurry to find Christ and get deeply into a good church before judgment falls. When you are converted, God promises to protect you and keep you safe from harm. You will then be raptured before the final judgments come.

Secondly, There Are Racial Signs

The words of Christ in Luke 21 continue:

> "Then he said to them, Nation (Greek *ethnos* or ethnic group) shall rise against nation (ethnic group), and kingdom (*Basilean* = national group) against kingdom (national group)" (Luke 21:10).

That's what we're seeing today. With all of our technology and science we don't seem to be able to stop ethnic strife between races, and wars between the nations.

President Clinton brought Arafat and Barak to Camp David near Washington. But he couldn't bring peace. When those men left Washington a few days later there was just as much tension between the ethnic groups and nations (Jews and Arabs) as ever. Clinton failed to bring peace to the Middle East. Only Christ can do that. And for all his political posturing, *Bill Clinton was not Jesus Christ!* Only when Christ Himself returns will He bring peace between all nations and ethnic groups. Clinton couldn't do that, and neither can George W. Bush. No human being can bring lasting peace on earth. Not even the coming Antichrist will be successful. *Only Jesus Christ will bring peace between the various races and ethnic groups and nations – when He comes back to the earth at the end of the Tribulation period. Only then will there be true peace on earth and good will toward all men!*

And we are preparing for His coming in our church here in Los Angeles. That's why every ethnic group and every race is welcome here. We love them and we want them here no matter what racial or

14

ethnic group they belong to. We are preparing for a day when all races and nations will come together in the Kingdom of Christ on this planet!

Thirdly, There Are Antisemitic Signs All Around Us

Many people hate the Jews, even through they are God's chosen people on earth (cf. Genesis 12:3). The passage in Luke 21 says:

> "And when ye shall see Jerusalem compassed (or circled around) with armies, then know that the desolation thereof is nigh (is near)" (Luke 21:20).

Antisemitism, hatred of the Jews, will grow so strong in the last days that great armies of Gentiles will come against Jerusalem and seek to destroy them, like Hitler did in World War II.

But the Jews are God's chosen people on earth according to the Bible:

> "They are beloved for the fathers' sakes" (Romans 11:28).

And Bible-believing Christians are strong supporters of Israel for that reason. But the Bible teaches that many others will turn against the Jewish people in the last days:

> "I will make Jerusalem a burdensome stone for all people" (Zechariah 12:3).

We can expect Antisemitism to increase even more in the future. It is a sign that we are now living in the days before the rapture. True Christians need to stand with Israel and the Jewish people in this darkening time of world history. A correct understanding of the New Testament makes it impossible for a true Christian to be an Antisemite. The hatred of the Jews which is predicted in the Bible will come as a result of ignorance, intolerance and unbelief.

Fourthly, There Are Religious Signs – Signs of Deception in False Religion

"And he said, Take heed that ye be not *deceived:* for many shall come in my name...go ye not therefore after them" (Luke 21:8).

In the Gospel of Matthew Christ added these words of warning:

"There shall arise false...prophets, and shall shew great signs and wonders; insomuch that, if it were possible, they shall *deceive* the very elect" (Matthew 24:24).

Much that we see on television and hear on the radio is religiously deceptive today. False religion reigns in many churches as well. The Bible says:

"For the time will come when they will not endure sound doctrine; but after their own lusts shall they heap to themselves teachers, having itching ears" (II Timothy 4:3).

Fifthly, There is the Sign of Religious Persecution

The persecution of Christians and Jews is going on throughout the world at an unprecedented rate. More Christians died for Christ in the twentieth century than in all the previous centuries combined.

Those who are true Christians have to meet secretly in Communist China. The *Los Angeles Times* (August 29, 2000, page A-11) gave this report of three Christians who were deported from China for sharing their faith:

China has deported three U.S. evangelists [Christians who witnessed to their faith] after detaining them in a round up of underground Protestant worshippers in central China, a rights group reported. The report...was accompanied by news that dozens of Chinese worshippers detained along with them have been sent to jail. An additional fifty followers of secret Protestant fellowships were arrested in three provinces, according

16

to the Hong Kong-based Information Center of Human
Rights and Democratic Movement in China.

Jesus predicted the worldwide persecution of Christians we see
going on today in China, Cuba, Viet Nam, the Sudan, the Moslem
nations, and elsewhere. He said,

> "They shall lay their hands on you, and persecute you,
> delivering you up...into prisons" (Luke 21:12).

Then He said that parents and relatives will often persecute you
if you become a real Christian. I have seen Christ's prediction
happen over and over during my forty-three years of ministry:

> "And ye shall be betrayed both by parents, and brethren,
> and kinsfolks, and friends...and ye shall be hated of all
> men for my name's sake" (Luke 21:16-17).

Jesus said that many of you have parents and friends who will
actually hate you if you become a real Christian.

First, they will try their best to get you not to go to a Bible-
believing church and become a zealous Christian. But if you do get
saved, they will turn on you and be very angry with you – for a time.
They usually get over it after several months, when they see that they
can't stop you.

But count the cost! Somebody won't like it if you become a real
Christian! Somebody will be against you – even in America! It costs
a great deal to become a true Christian in these dark times! It's a sign
that we are living in the period before the rapture.

Finally, Christ Gave Us a Sixth Sign to Show Us We Are Near the End. I Call it the Psychological Sign

Jesus said:

> "Take heed (pay attention) to yourselves, lest at any time
> your hearts be overcharged (weighed down, or
> weighted down) with...(the) cares (anxieties) of this
> life, and so that day come upon you unawares. For as a

snare shall it come on all them that dwell on the face of
the whole earth" (Luke 21:34-35).

One young man who came a few times to our church said, "I
can't come back next Sunday. I have to help my aunt move." He had
six days to do it, but it "had" to happen on Sunday morning. He was
weighed down with the problems of life. Many miss church for other
light and foolish reasons. They too are weighed down with the cares
of this life. And that day will come upon them unawares.

You may get past drugs and sex, but later get weighed down
with family problems that suck you under. I have seen that happen to
many young couples across the years.

And then Jesus said:

> "*Watch ye therefore, and pray always,* that ye may be
> accounted worthy to escape all these things that shall
> come to pass, and to stand before the Son of man"
> (Luke 21:36).

To be ready for the end of the world and the Judgment to come, there
are three things you need to do:

(1) Come into a good local church. Nothing else will help you if
you don't do that.

(2) Come to Christ. He died for your sins. He rose literally and
physically from the dead. He is alive at the right hand of
God. He is there for you now. Come to Him.

(3) Not only do you need to come into the church and come to
Christ, but you also need to pray. Jesus said that prayer is the
key to living a successful Christian life in the last days.

Is America "Losing It"?

Do you think I have been too harsh and blunt in this chapter?
Nothing else has helped our churches or our nation. I think it is time
for someone to speak out strongly. It should have been done long ago.

As I sit here alone in my study tonight, two national news
magazines lie on the desk in front of me, their covers leering at me in
the soft light.

The cover of *U.S. News and World Report* has these words, in large, bold letters: *"Drowning in Debt."* The accompanying article asks, "How did America get into this mess, spending away our future earnings?" Nearly everyone I know is worried about money. What will happen when our house of credit cards comes crashing down?

The cover of *Time* has a kid's backpack on it with a pistol sticking out. In large letters are the words: *"The Columbine Effect."* Inside is a story of yet another fifteen-year-old high school killer. The article says, "Once again, a lost boy shoots up his school and rattles our psyches." High schools across our nation are becoming dangerous jungles of crime, violence, and sin.

How many brains does it take to see that America is "losing it"? How much farther can we go before our whole way of life crumbles? *There are many sociological signs around us that show we are in the last days. The rapture will come soon, and you will be left behind.*

CHAPTER THREE

TURMOIL IN ISRAEL AND THE COMING THIRD TEMPLE

> "Let no man deceive you by any means: for that day shall not come, except there come a falling away first, and that man of sin be revealed, the son of perdition; who opposeth and exalteth himself above all that is called God, or that is worshipped; so that he as God sitteth in the temple of God, shewing himself that he is God" (II Thessalonians 2:3-4).

On September 28, 2000, an Israeli political leader, Ariel Sharon, visited the Temple Mount area in Jerusalem. A Moslem shrine occupies this site where the Jewish Temple once stood. It is against Moslem law for a Jew to enter the area. Sharon's visit sparked riots by Moslems throughout Israel. *USA Today* featured a photograph on the front page which showed Moslems burning an Israeli flag during a riot in Gaza City. The headline read, ISRAELI MILITARY POISED FOR WAR.

The violence subsided, but the fact remains: Moslems do not want Jews in the area where the Temple once stood. At the same time the Jews are looking forward to rebuilding the Temple on this site, as the Bible predicts both in the Old Testament book of Ezekiel and in II Thessalonians 2:4 in the New Testament.

The big question is this: how can the Jews rebuild the Temple on the site of this Moslem mosque, since it can't be built anywhere else? Even a brief visit to this area by Ariel Sharon nearly started a war. But the Bible predicts that events will change in the future.

The Coming Antichrist Will Make a Treaty With Israel That Will Give the Jews the Temple Area

The Bible teaches that the Antichrist will be the final ruler of the world. Dr. Herman Hoyt points out that this demagogue is given eight titles in the New Testament, including "false Christ," "the man

20

of sin," "the lawless one," "the Antichrist" and "the beast" (cf. Herman A. Hoyt, *The End Times*, Moody Press, 1969, p. 119). The Antichrist will become the most powerful ruler the world has ever known.

Dr. Hoyt tells us how the Antichrist will give the Temple area to the Jews:

> He will make a treaty with the Jews in his own name (John 5:43), which will bring them into possession of the temple area where they can renew their long discontinued worship (Revelation 11:1-3). (Ibid., p. 128).

The signing of this treaty will mark the beginning of the seven-year Tribulation period (Daniel 9:27).

The Rebuilt Temple Will Then Be Taken Over By the Antichrist

The Jews will rebuild the Temple and reinstate animal sacrifices with the Antichrist's help. He will then break his covenant with them. The Temple sacrifices and worship will be stopped. The Antichrist will deify himself, proclaiming that he is God, and demand that divine honor and worship be paid to him (II Thessalonians 2:4).

Then the Antichrist will arrange for a huge statue of himself to be placed in the Temple area, and order mankind to worship this image (Revelation 13:14-15; Matthew 24:15). *At this time the Jews will realize that this is the "abomination of desolation" spoken of in Daniel 9:27 and 12:11.* Jesus said, "...ye therefore shall see the abomination of desolation, spoken of by Daniel the prophet, stand in the holy place" (Matthew 24:15). These words of Christ reveal that the Temple and its "holy place" (i.e. the Holy of Holies) will indeed be rebuilt and then desecrated.

Dr. Richard W. DeHaan wrote:

> Scripture passages, including II Thessalonians 2:4 and Revelation 13:14-18, indicate that an image will be erected by the coming Antichrist, and that refusal to worship this idol will trigger a period of dreadful

persecution, primarily for the Jews, but for all the other inhabiters of the earth as well (Richard DeHaan, *Israel and the Nations in Prophecy*, Zondervan Publishing House, 1968, p. 89).

That's what the Bible is talking about in II Thessalonians 2:3-4,

> "Let no man deceive you by any means: for that day shall not come, except there come a falling away first, and that man of sin be revealed, the son of perdition; who opposeth and exalteth himself above all that is called God, or that is worshipped; so that he as God sitteth in the temple of God, shewing himself that he is God" (II Thessalonians 2:3-4).

Take the first phrase, "Let no man deceive you by any means: for that day shall not come, except there come a falling away first..." (II Thessalonians 2:3). This tells us there will be a great apostasy (falling away) among "Christians." I believe that we are going through the beginning of this period right now. It is a time of confusion and unbelief in the churches of Christendom. The words translated "a falling away" could be translated "the apostasy." In the last one hundred and fifty years, since Charles G. Finney began his ministry, the great Protestant and Baptist groups have experienced unprecedented apostasy. The denominations have largely turned away from the Bible as the God's authoritative Word. Most church members are lost. I believe that we are living in the first half of II Thessalonians 2:3 right now! *We are in the great apostasy!*

Then the verse continues, "...and that man of sin be revealed, the son of perdition" (II Thessalonians 2:3). This refers to the Antichrist. He will be "revealed" in the future, when he suddenly appears and rather quickly becomes the universal ruler of the world.

Verse four tells us that this man "opposeth and exalteth himself above all that is called God, or that is worshipped..." (II Thessalonians 2:4a). His true nature will come out – he will be against God and His Son, Jesus Christ. That is why he is called "the Antichrist" in the First and Second Epistles of John. The word "antichrist" has two parts. "Anti" means "against," and then "Christ." So the name "Antichrist" means "against Christ." This man will be against Jesus Christ because he, himself will desire to be worshipped in the place of the Triune God of Scripture (II Thessalonians 2:4a).

The passage ends with these words, "So that he as God sitteth in the temple of God, shewing himself that he is God" (II Thessalonians 2:4b). He will enter the rebuilt Temple in Jerusalem and declare himself to be God.

You may say, "Why would anyone believe that a mere man is Almighty God?" The answer is given in II Thessalonians 2:11-12,

> "For this cause *God shall send them strong delusion, that they should believe a lie:* that they all might be damned who believed not the truth, but had pleasure in unrighteousness" (II Thessalonians 2:11-12).

God will punish the unbelieving world by sending "strong delusion." The word "strong" is from the Greek "energion" (strong, effective). The second word "delusion" is from the Greek word "plané," which means "a straying from orthodoxy, deception, error, delusion" (*Strong's Concordance*). So, God Himself will punish people by sending them a strong, effective spirit of error.

This is called "judicial judgment." It is what happened to the Romans in ancient times (Romans 1:24,26,28). It is what will happen to *you* if you go on fooling around like you've been doing: "God gave them over to a reprobate mind" (Romans 1:28). And when God gives up on you and punishes you by permanently blinding you spiritually, then you can never be saved.

You can only go on so long living in sin – getting drunk and dancing and drugging yourself. You can only go on so long missing church on Sunday. Soon God will say, "That's enough! He crossed over the deadline. He went too long and too far. I'm giving up on him. I'm giving up on her." When that happens it's forever too late for you to get saved. God will send *you* "strong delusion that (you) should believe a lie."

When God gives up on you, you will spend the rest of your life believing Satan's lies concerning religion – until you die and go to Hell.

> "They shall go...to seek the Lord; but they shall not find him; he hath withdrawn himself from them"
> (Hosea 5:6).

John Lennon once said the Beatles were more popular than Jesus Christ, and that they would eventually replace Christ. Hundreds of thousands of young people believed John Lennon's lie – just as people in the future will believe the Antichrist. They will believe a lie. They will be given up to reprobation as a result. They will then worship a man instead of God. All of this will happen after the third Temple is built in Jerusalem.

The following events are prophesied:

1. The Antichrist will make a treaty with Israel.
2. The Antichrist will then break that treaty, go into the Temple and proclaim that he, himself is God.

The Events in the Second Half of the Tribulation Will Then Unfold

The Tribulation is the coming seven-year period in which the Antichrist will rule the world. The revival predicted in Revelation 7:4-14 will take place in the first half of the Tribulation. After the Antichrist proclaims that he is God, great persecution will occur against Christians. At this point "God shall send them strong delusion, that they should believe a lie" (II Thessalonians 2:11). The revival will cease, and those who remain unsaved will be given up by God. Several other negative events will occur in the second half of the Tribulation.

First, the wrath of Satan will be fully unleashed on mankind:

> "And there was war in heaven: Michael and his angels fought against the dragon (Satan); and the dragon fought and his angels, And prevailed not; neither was their place found any more in heaven. And the great dragon was cast out, that old serpent, called the Devil, and Satan, which deceiveth the whole world: he was cast out into the earth, and his angels (i.e. demons) were cast out with him" (Revelation 12:7-9).

> "Woe to the inhabiters of the earth and of the sea! for the devil is come down unto you, having great wrath,

because he knoweth that he hath but a short time"
(Revelation 12:12).

Right now Satan can come and go into God's presence in Heaven
(Job 1:6-12). But at this point in the Tribulation he will be totally
barred from the throne of God. This will enrage him into goading the
Antichrist (the Beast) to force the world to worship his image and to
blaspheme God:

> "And he opened his mouth in blasphemy against God, to
> blaspheme his name, and his tabernacle, and them that
> dwell in heaven. And it was given unto him to make
> war with the saints, and to overcome them: and power
> was given him over all kindreds, and tongues, and
> nations. And all that dwell upon the earth shall worship
> him, whose names are not written in the book of life of
> the Lamb slain from the foundation of the world"
> (Revelation 13:6-8).

The Devil will be so infuriated that he will move the Antichrist
to "make war" against every Christian living on earth and he will
"overcome them" (Revelation 13:7). It will be a virtual blood bath,
with hundreds of thousands of Christians martyred.

Count the cost! It will cost you something to become a *real*
Christian! It may cost you your very life!

The Bottomless Pit Opened

Then, secondly, the bottomless pit will be opened (Revelation
9:1). Thousands of new demons will pour forth from this pit. Some
of them are in the air about us now. But at that time all the demons
will be loosed. There will be even more demonic activity than there
is now! (Revelation 9:1-12). Demon power will be so great that
people will think about suicide constantly (Revelation 9:6). All of
this is coming very soon! People will have suicidal thoughts day and
night as a result of demonic torment.

Dr. John R. Rice told this story from the days when he was in
the Army:

25

During World War I, one time I did guard duty over some criminally insane in a hospital. One poor, troubled, demented man would put his thumbs in his eyes and try to pull them out, and we frantically pulled his hands away. He would pull out his hair by handfuls until his head was perfectly bald. At the midnight hour I sat near his cot with an Enfield rifle, on guard duty. He whispered to me, "Leave your gun there for just a little bit and go out in the hall. Go for a drink of water. I promise I won't hurt anybody else but myself. Oh, give me a chance to kill myself!" He pleaded with me (to) shoot him, he was in such torment (John R. Rice, ***Behold, He Cometh!***, Sword of the Lord, 1977, page 171).

That's the way people will be during this time because of such intense activity by Satan and his demons.

The Bowl Judgments

Third, God will pour out seven "vials" or bowls of wrath and judgment on the world.

"And I heard a great voice out of the temple saying to the seven angels, Go your ways, and pour out the vials of the wrath of God upon the earth.

The first bowl.

And the first went, and poured out his vial upon the earth; and there fell a noisome and grievous sore upon the men which had the mark of the beast, and upon them which worshipped his image.

The second bowl.

And the second angel poured out his vial upon the sea; and it became as the blood of a dead man: and every living soul died in the sea.

The third bowl.

And the third angel poured out his vial upon the rivers and fountains of waters; and they became blood. And I heard the angel of the waters say, Thou art righteous, O Lord, which art, and wast, and shalt be, because thou hast judged thus. For they have shed the blood of saints and prophets, and thou hast given them blood to drink; for they are worthy. And I heard another out of the altar say, Even so, Lord God Almighty, true and righteous are thy judgments.

The fourth bowl.

And the fourth angel poured out his vial upon the sun; and power was given unto him to scorch men with fire. And men were scorched with great heat, and blasphemed the name of God, which hath power over these plagues: and they repented not to give him glory.

The fifth bowl.

And the fifth angel poured out his vial upon the seat of the beast; and his kingdom was full of darkness; and they gnawed their tongues for pain, And blasphemed the God of heaven because of their pains and their sores, and repented not of their deeds.

The sixth bowl.

And the sixth angel poured out his vial upon the great river Euphrates; and the water thereof was dried up, that the way of the kings of the east might be prepared.

The Gathering of the World's Armies at Armageddon.

And I saw three unclean spirits like frogs come out of the mouth of the dragon, and out of the mouth of the beast, and out of the mouth of the false prophet. For they are the spirits of devils, working miracles, which go forth unto the kings of the earth and of the whole world, to gather them to the battle of that great day of God Almighty. Behold, I come as a thief. Blessed is he that watcheth, and keepeth his garments, lest he walk naked, and they see his shame. And he gathered them together into a place called in the Hebrew tongue Armageddon.

The seventh bowl.

And the seventh angel poured out his vial into the air; and there came a great voice out of the temple of heaven, from the throne, saying, It is done. And there were voices, and thunders, and lightnings; and there was a great earthquake, such as was not since men were upon the earth, so mighty an earthquake, and so great. And the great city was divided into three parts, and the cities of the nations fell: and great Babylon came in remembrance before God, to give unto her the cup of the wine of the fierceness of his wrath. And every island fled away, and the mountains were not found. And there fell upon men a great hail out of heaven, every stone about the weight of a talent: and men blasphemed God because of the plague of the hail; for the plague thereof was exceeding great." (Revelation 16:1-21)

The Unpardonable Sin

Fourthly, there's an important application of all of this to the life of every unconverted person. The passage of Scripture we've studied, in II Thessalonians 2, tells us that we are now in the apostasy. This will be followed by the rise of the Antichrist, the rebuilding of the Jewish Temple, and the Antichrist's proclamation of himself as God.

"For the mystery of iniquity doth already work: only he who now letteth ("hindereth," Scofield) will let ("hinder," Scofield), until he be taken out of the way" (II Thessalonians 2:7).

This shows that God "restrains" the events of the Tribulation. He "hinders" or holds them back. That's why World War III hasn't broken out in the Middle East. That's why everything quiets down again after each uprising around the Temple area in Jerusalem. But notice the end of II Thessalonians 2:7, "...until he be taken out of the way." The Holy Spirit will not be **removed** (as some falsely teach), but will rather **not be "in the way" anymore!** When God **steps aside**, all these events will come crashing down on the world-scene.

Evangelical commentator John MacArthur says:

> It must be God's power in operation that holds back Satan, so that the man of sin, the son of destruction, won't be able to come until God permits it by removing his restraining power (**MacArthur Study Bible**, note on II Thessalonians 2:6).

It often **seems** like these events are going to happen right away! There's a turmoil, bombings, fighting. Then everything returns to normal. We have seen that happen over and over in Jerusalem.

But one of these days God is going to step aside. He will get "out of the way." Then mankind will be plunged into the Great Tribulation.

Now notice II Thessalonians 2:11,

> "And for this cause God shall send them strong delusion, that they should believe a lie" (II Thessalonians 2:11).

The previous verse tells us that God sends "strong delusion" because "they received not the love of the truth, that they might be saved" (II Thessalonians 2:10b). They refuse salvation, so God sends them strong delusion "that they should believe a lie."

That's a prophetic picture of people committing the unpardonable sin in the Tribulation period. Dr. John R. Rice said,

> Those who take the mark of the beast thereby commit the unpardonable sin and doom themselves forever in Hell...in the Great Tribulation, yet future, men will cross the deadline, will commit the unpardonable sin (**Crossing the Deadline**, Sword of the Lord, 1953, pp. 16, 11).

What is the unpardonable sin? Dr. John R. Rice explains it:

> The unpardonable sin is such a sin as any man or woman might commit after great enlightenment, after

many calls (to salvation) are refused, after many
pleadings of the Holy Spirit are mocked and resisted
and insulted (Ibid., p. 17). The sinner (committing the
unpardonable sin) becomes hardened, set against God,
against salvation, and so will never repent (Ibid., p. 24).
God's Spirit does not call the forsaken sinner (Ibid., p.
25). The man who has set his heart against God forever
and has insulted and driven away the Holy Spirit will
never come for the cleansing which is offered (Ibid.).
So one who has driven away the Spirit of God and has
passed the boundaries of mercy cannot repent (Ibid.).

*You can commit the unpardonable sin right now! In fact, you
are in great danger of committing the unpardonable sin.* When you
commit it, you can never be saved. You may live for many years, but
God will give up on you for ever if you step over the line and He is
"taken out of the way" in your life (II Thessalonians 2:7).

When that happens, God will give you "over to a reprobate
mind" (Romans 1:28). *Given up by God! You can never be
converted!*

"...because they received not the love of the truth, that
they might be saved. And for this cause God shall send
them strong delusion, that they should believe a lie:
That they all might be damned who believed not the
truth" (II Thessalonians 2:10-12).

One young man said to me, "I'm not as interested in becoming a
Christian as I was before I heard your sermons. I wanted to hear you
preach at the beginning, but I am less and less interested now." He
was trying to make it sound like my sermons were too poor to
convince him. But I know his case. The fact is he rejected the truth,
so God slowly began to reject him.

Since I wrote the previous paragraph, it appears that God has
given up on him completely. He now has no interest in Christianity
at all.

"And even as they did not like to retain God in their
knowledge, God gave them over to a reprobate
mind..." (Romans 1:28).

30

And God will give you up also if you wait too long – until your heart is hardened and you are reprobate.

> You have waited so flippantly, refused Him so lightly,
> You have sinned long and dreadfully, your heart is so wrong;
> Oh if God grows impatient, the sweet Spirit offended,
> If no longer He calls you, doom is yours when He's gone.
>
> Then how sad facing judgment you'll recall with no mercy,
> That you tarried and lingered till the Spirit was gone;
> What reproaches and mourning if when death finds you hopeless,
> You have tarried and lingered and have waited too long!
> ("If You Linger Too Long," by Dr. John R. Rice, 1895-1980).

Oh God, I'm Not Ready to Die!

Dr. John R. Rice once told about a man who came to hear him preach night after night in evangelistic meetings. The man sat at the back and laughed and mocked at the sermons. Then the evangelist moved on and the meetings were over. The years passed but the man never did get saved.

One night Dr. Rice spoke with his sister on the telephone. She said, "John, do you remember Mr. (So and so)?" He said, "Yes. I remember that he came to the services, but he didn't get saved. He mocked and joked and laughed about the sermons."

Then Dr. Rice's sister told him what happened to that man. He got sick to the stomach and they took him to the doctor. The doctor said, "It's too late. There's nothing I can do. Go home and write a will. You won't live long." He had peritonitis.

It was hot that summer in Dallas. It was before they had air conditioning. They left the windows open to let in a little breeze. That man lay in his house dying for weeks. No one could comfort him. They sent for a Baptist preacher, but he couldn't seem to lead the man to Christ. As he lay there dying, he kept telling those who came to see him that it was too late, he had waited too long.

They say you could hear him shouting for blocks during those hot summer nights in Dallas. They say you could hear him screaming, ***"Oh God, I need more time! Oh God, I'm not ready to***

die! Oh, God, I'm not ready to die! I'm not ready to die! I'm not ready to die!"

And that's the way you will die if you go on rejecting Jesus Christ – until it's too late for you to be saved. You will then be left behind to be judged by God in the Tribulation.

> "And for this cause God shall send them strong delusion, that they should believe a lie: That they all might be damned who believe not the truth" (II Thessalonians 2:11-12).

CHAPTER FOUR

THE GREAT FALLING AWAY TODAY

"Let no man deceive you by any means: for that day
shall not come, except there come a falling away first,
and that man of sin be revealed, the son of perdition"
(II Thessalonians 2:3).

In his book *The Vanishing Ministry* Woodrow Kroll points out
that each year between 3,500 and 4,000 U.S. churches close their
doors forever. The mainline denominations lose thousands of
members annually. And pollster George Barna declares, "Born Again
Christians Ignorant of Faith" (*Baptist Bible Tribune*, April 15, 1996,
p. 28). I believe these are signs that we are now in the last days.

Today's apostasy did not come about suddenly. It had a
beginning and growth in history, leading up to the apostate church of
the Tribulation.

Deep in the Apostasy

I am convinced that we are now, at this time, living deep in the
apostasy spoken of in II Thessalonians 2:3. The apostasy started with
the ministry of Charles G. Finney in the 1820s. It grew across
seventeen decades into the monstrous condition we see in the
churches today.

I have dealt with this subject at length in two books, titled
Preaching to a Dying Nation and *Today's Apostasy: How
"Decisionism" is Destroying Our Churches.* You can phone me at
(818)352-0452 to order these books. They should be read by those
who wish to have a more comprehensive study of this subject.

What Did the Apostasy Produce?

First, the apostasy produced many professing Christians who are
not actually converted. The Scofield headline to II Timothy 3:1-7
says, "The apostasy predicted." Then the passage is given:

33

"This know also, that in the last days perilous times shall come. For men shall be lovers of their own selves, covetous, boasters, proud, blasphemers, disobedient to parents, unthankful, unholy, without natural affection, trucebreakers, false accusers, incontinent, fierce, despisers of those that are good, traitors, heady, highminded, lovers of pleasures more than lovers of God; having a form of godliness, but denying the power thereof: from such turn away. For of this sort are they which creep into houses, and lead captive silly women laden with sins, led away with divers lusts, ever learning, and never able to come to the knowledge of the truth."

Floods of Lost People Pour Into the Churches

Second, the apostasy produced multitudes of lost people in the churches who will not endure sound doctrine. That is, they will not endure preaching against sin; they will not put up with preaching which contains reproving, rebuking and exhorting:

"Preach the word; be instant in season, out of season; reprove, rebuke, exhort with all longsuffering and doctrine. For the time will come when they will not endure sound doctrine; but after their own lusts shall they heap to themselves teachers, having itching ears; and they shall turn away their ears from the truth, and shall be turned unto fables" (II Timothy 4:2-4).

The Bible says, "Preach the word...reprove, rebuke, exhort" (II Timothy 4:2). One verse later, we are given this prophetic warning, "For the time will come when they will not endure sound doctrine (reproving, rebuking and exhorting); but after their own lusts shall they heap to themselves teachers, having itching ears" (II Timothy 4:3).

Mystery Babylon – The Great False "Church" of the Last Days

Third, the apostasy prepares the way for Mystery Babylon – the great whore – the false church of the end-times.

"And upon her forehead was a name written,
MYSTERY, BABYLON THE GREAT, THE
MOTHER OF HARLOTS AND ABOMINATIONS
OF THE EARTH" (Revelation 17:5).

"And he cried mightily with a strong voice, saying,
Babylon the great is fallen, is fallen, and is become the
habitation of devils, and the hold of every foul spirit,
and a cage of every unclean and hateful bird"
(Revelation 18:2).

The Scofield note on Revelation 18:2 says, "Babylon, 'confusion,' is
repeatedly used by the prophets in a symbolic sense...Two Babylons
are to be distinguished in Revelation: [the first is] ecclesiastical
Babylon, which is apostate Christendom...Ecclesiastical Babylon is
'the great whore' (Revelation 17:1)." I am convinced that we are
seeing this formation of apostate Christianity right now, today.
Revelation 18:2 says that these false churches "become the habitation
of devils, and the hold of every foul spirit, and a cage of every
unclean and hateful bird." That is a picture of countless mainline,
evangelical, charismatic, and even more conservative churches in our
day, since vast multitudes in these congregations remain unconverted.
Fourth, the apostasy creates false Christians who make life
difficult for those who are truly converted:

"Then shall they deliver you up to be afflicted, and shall
kill you: and ye shall be hated of all nations for my
name's sake. And then shall many be offended, and
shall betray one another, and shall hate one another.
And many false prophets shall rise, and shall deceive
many. And because iniquity shall abound, the love of
many shall wax cold" (Matthew 24:9-12).

Fifth, the apostasy produces professing Christians who are only
interested in material things:

"But as the days of Noe (Noah) were, so shall also the
coming of the Son of man be. For as in the days that
were before the flood they were eating and drinking,
marrying and giving in marriage, until the day that Noe
(Noah) entered into the ark, and knew not until the

35

flood came, and took them all away; so shall also the coming of the Son of man be" (Matthew 24:37-39).

I do not know how few the number of truly born again Christians is, but the number seems pitifully small:

"Except the Lord of hosts had left unto us a very small remnant, we should have been as Sodom, and we should have been like unto Gomorrah" (Isaiah 1:9).

Jesus said:

"But as the days of Noe (Noah) were, so shall also the coming of the Son of man be" (Matthew 24:37).

Why Did the Apostasy Come About?

As it was in the days of Noah, many today have called on the name of the Lord without being converted. In Genesis 4:26 we are told:

"And to Seth, to him also there was born a son; and he called his name Enos: then began men to call upon the name of the Lord" (Genesis 4:26).

But even though they had called on the name of the Lord, they were unsaved:

"And the Lord said, My spirit shall not always strive with man, for that he also is flesh: yet his days shall be an hundred and twenty years" (Genesis 6:3).

"The earth also was corrupt before God, and the earth was filled with violence. And God looked upon the earth, and, behold, it was corrupt; for all flesh had corrupted his way upon the earth. And God said unto Noah, The end of all flesh is come before me; for the earth is filled with violence through them; and, behold, I will destroy them with the earth" (Genesis 6:11-13).

How many people actually got into the Ark and were saved? Only eight (II Peter 2:5a). The rest of "the ungodly" went to Hell (II Peter 2:5b). They experienced eternal damnation even though they had called on the name of the Lord (Genesis 4:26). It does no good to pray or "believe" without getting into the Ark, a type or illustration of Christ. Many today have said a "sinner's prayer," believed a doctrine, or made a Lordship "decision" without getting into the Ark! They have experienced "decisionism" instead of "conversion."

Here are working definitions of the two terms "decisionism" and "conversion":

> *Decisionism* is the belief that a person is saved by coming forward, raising the hand, saying a prayer, believing a doctrine, making a Lordship commitment, or some other external, human act, which is taken as the equivalent to, and proof of, the miracle of inward conversion; it is the belief that a person is saved through the agency of a merely external decision; the belief that performing one of these human actions shows that a person is saved.

> *Conversion* is the result of that work of the Holy Spirit which draws a lost sinner to Jesus Christ for justification and regeneration, and changes the sinner's standing before God from lost to saved, imparting divine life to the depraved soul, thus producing a new direction in the life of the convert. The objective side of salvation is justification. The subjective side of salvation is regeneration. The result is conversion.

Conversion was changed into decisionism largely through the ministry and writings of Charles G. Finney. His views engulfed the evangelical churches of America, and later, in the twentieth century, infiltrated most churches in the British Isles.

Liberalism Not the Cause of Apostasy

Finney's decisionism first ruined the Congregationalists, then the Methodists, then the Presbyterians, and then the various Baptist groups. *Liberalism did __not__ produce apostasy in these churches –*

decisionism did. Decisionism *produced* liberalism. Every liberal professor in one of the seminaries I attended had made some sort of decision. But these decisions did not convert them – so they went headlong into liberalism when they studied it. Decisionism produces liberalism because an unconverted person, though he has made a decision, simply cannot understand the spiritual message of the Bible (cf. I Corinthians 2:14). Jesus once said to a famous Bible teacher, "Marvel not that I said unto thee, Ye must be born again" (John 3:7).

No matter who you are, what you have learned, how many "decisions" or "rededications" you have made, or how much you have tried to make Christ your Lord, you still must experience conversion or you will go to Hell (Matthew 18:3).

Make *very* sure that you are not lost when the rapture comes. Do not be shut out of the Ark, as the people in Noah's day were.

> In times like these, you need a Saviour,
> In times like these, you need an anchor.
> Be very sure, be very sure
> Your anchor holds and grips the Solid Rock.
>
> This Rock is Jesus, yes, He's the One;
> This Rock is Jesus, the only One!
> Be very sure, be very sure,
> Your anchor holds and grips the Solid Rock!
> ("In Times Like These" by Ruth Caye Jones, 1944).

CHAPTER FIVE

THE RAPTURE!

"For the Lord himself shall descend from heaven with a shout, with the voice of the archangel, and with the trump of God: and the dead in Christ shall rise first: Then we which are alive and remain shall be caught up together with them in the clouds, to meet the Lord in the air: and so shall we ever be with the Lord. Wherefore comfort one another with these words"
(I Thessalonians 4:16-18).

How near is the rapture? That's a question people have been inquiring about for generations. The Disciples asked Jesus, "What shall be the sign of thy coming, and of the end of the world (age)?" (Matthew 24:3).

On two different occasions Christ cautioned them against speculating about the exact time (Matthew 24:36; Acts 1:7). But He did give them a number of signs that would indicate the general period. He said,

"When these things begin to come to pass, then look up, and lift up your heads; for your redemption draweth nigh" (Luke 21:28).

All the signs Christ gave us are now visible on the world scene. It therefore appears that we are moving toward the end of history and the rapture. Here are six of the most important signs that we are nearing the time of the end:

1. The reestablishing of Israel in 1948, with the Jewish people returning to their God-given homeland (Luke 21:24; Matthew 24:32-34; Ezekiel 37:21; 38:8).

2. The rise of the "common market," a coalition of European nations moving toward union (Daniel 2:40-45; Revelation 17:12).

3. The increase of worldwide persecution against Christians and Jews (Matthew 24:9-10; Jeremiah 30:7; Daniel 12:1).

4. The increase of worldwide famines, imbalanced ecology, pestilences like the AIDS epidemic, and an increasing number of earthquakes (Matthew 24:7).

5. The rise of apostasy in Christianity (II Thessalonians 2:3; Matthew 24:11-12).

6. The return of mankind to conditions like those that prevailed in the days of Noah, before the great Flood (Matthew 24:37-39).

The breakdown of society, and other prophetic signs, are constantly in the news, and in our daily experiences.

When Billy Graham received the Congressional Gold Medal from the United States Congress, he said:

> We are a society poised on the brink of self-destruction. Our culture is plagued with crime and violence, drug abuse, racial and ethnic tension, broken families and corruption.

Dr. Woodrow Kroll, the director of Back to the Bible, tells us that between 3,500 and 4,000 churches close their doors forever each year in the United States. Many other churches are struggling to keep the doors open.

I spoke with a young man from the Hmong tribe in Cambodia on the telephone recently. People in the Hmong tribe are experiencing tremendous revival in Cambodia and Viet Nam. But this young man is an exchange student here in the United States, in one of our eastern colleges. He had heard about my book, *Today's Apostasy*, on a radio program in Minnesota. When he phoned to ask about the book, he told me he sensed that something is wrong in America, that many so-called "Christians" here seem lifeless and dead compared to the revival he has experienced first-hand in the jungles of Cambodia. I had to agree with him. These are dark and discouraging times for true believers in many parts of the world.

Faithful Christians in the Western world try to get unchurched neighbors and friends to come on Sunday. But it's hard to get people to listen nowadays, because most people won't make a commitment to be in church every week. Little things come up which seem more important to them than being in church.

I don't care how many Bible verses you know, or how many prayers you've prayed, if you don't love being in a good church every Sunday, I think you are still lost.

A few Sundays ago over twenty-six thousand people ran half naked through the streets of Los Angeles during the traditional hour of Christian worship, in the annual marathon. As these wild neo-pagans ran through our city streets, we huddled in church. Only a small number of people are real Christians at this dark, pagan hour of world history.

Is there any hope? Is there any way out of the darkness? I have to give a resounding "yes" to those questions. Yes, there *is* hope! But it will not come from man. Our hope lies in things only God can do: revival, the rapture of true Christians, and the second coming of Christ!

The Events of the Rapture

Think for a moment about this event called "the rapture." I Thessalonians 4:16-18 tells us a great deal about it.

1. Christ will descend from Heaven. The passage says:

   "The Lord himself shall descend from heaven with a shout..."

2. But He will not come all the way down to earth. The passage says:

   "to meet the Lord in the air..."

3. There will be a loud "shout," and a trumpet will blow as Christ comes down in the air:

   "with the voice of the archangel, and with the trump (trumpet) of God..."

41

4. The true Christians who have already died will be resurrected and lifted up in the sky (i.e. raptured):

    "And the dead in Christ shall rise first..."

5. Then those true Christians who are still living will be raptured also, lifted up in the air to meet Jesus. The passage says:

    "Then we which are alive and remain shall
    be caught up together with them in the
    clouds, to meet the Lord in the air..."

These are the five tremendous truths of the rapture. The hope of true Christians lies in the resurrection of the living and the dead through Jesus Christ, who said:

"I go to prepare a place for you. And if I go and prepare
a place for you, I will come again, and receive you unto
myself; that where I am, there ye may be also"
(John 14:2-3).

The Comfort of the Rapture

I Thessalonians 4:16-18 concludes by saying:

"Wherefore comfort one another with these words"
(I Thessalonians 4:18).

For the truly converted Christian, there is great comfort and encouragement in this promise of God.

Think how horrible it is for lost people when a relative dies. They look at the dead body. They think, "I will never see my loved one again." Their hearts ache with bitter hopelessness. They watch the coffin lowered into a black hole in the ground. They hear the dirt falling on the lid of the casket. They think about the body rotting, full of worms, under the ground. They think about their own body being buried like that some day. They are filled with terrific horror, helplessness and despair. *The Bible calls them "others which have no hope"* (I Thessalonians 4:13). *The Bible speaks of them as "having no hope, and without God in the world"* (Ephesians 2:12).

How about you? Do you have the hope of eternal life? Do you have assurance that your dead body will rise to meet Christ in the air?

> "Thy dead men shall live, together with my dead body shall they arise. Awake and sing, ye that dwell in dust...and the earth shall cast out the dead" (Isaiah 26:19).

Only Christ can give you the hope of resurrection. That's why you need to turn to Him fully and wholeheartedly today. And turning to Christ begins by your commitment to be in a Bible-believing church every Sunday. And it isn't enough to go once in a while, when it's convenient. That won't help you at all. You need to make a commitment to be there *every Sunday and never miss* – no matter what comes up. That's the only thing that will help you get converted. You see, if you don't attend a gospel-preaching church you're probably not going to get saved. You need to hear the gospel as often as possible. That's one main reason you need to be there every Sunday. Then you'll have a wonderful chance of getting saved. Being in a good church on a regular basis is the first step.

And then examine yourself inwardly. See how wicked and sinful you are by nature. Come to distrust your own heart and hate the evil in your depraved mind and emotions. Give up all trust in yourself. Stop depending on your own feelings and thoughts. Come to hate your sin. Come to the place of distrusting your own sinful heart.

> "The heart is deceitful above all things, and desperately wicked" (Jeremiah 17:9).

Knowing this, you should throw yourself on Jesus Christ for mercy. He is the Son of God. He died on the Cross so your filthiness could be cleansed, so your sins could be washed away by His Blood. And He is alive in Heaven now, on the right side of God. Come to Jesus, and believe in Him fully, and your sins will be washed away. You'll be ready for the rapture!

The Warning in the Rapture

There is also a warning in the rapture, and it is this: if Christ comes and you are not converted, you will be left behind! Dr. Tim LaHaye has several books on that subject which have repeatedly been on the *New York Times* bestseller list. More people are reading the "Left Behind" series than any other books in America. Will you be left behind when the rapture comes?

This won't be a pleasant world after the rapture. God's bowl judgments will be poured out on a planet in rebellion. Mankind will be under great judgment. The world will become much more frightening than it is now. *I would not want to be left behind if I were you!*

People will have incurable sores on their bodies. They will wander about searching for something to drink, but the world's water supply will be poisoned. And many other horrors will come on earth soon after the rapture (ref. Revelation 16:1-21).

I would *not* want to be here when God pours out these judgments on the world. I would want to be raptured if I were you. I would want to have my sins washed away in Christ's Blood so I could go to Heaven. I would prepare to meet God now if I were you. The Bible says, "Prepare to meet thy God" (Amos 4:12).

First, get into a Bible-believing church every Sunday. Make that an important part of your weekly schedule. Stop fooling around with God. Be in a gospel-preaching church every Sunday.

Second, listen hard to the sermons. Let God bring you under conviction of sin. Let Him show you that you are lost. Think of how your sin is poisoning you, how it is ruining your life, and how it will damn you in eternity.

Third, think about Jesus Christ. Think about how He can cleanse your sins with His Blood, and give you a whole new life in the local church.

CHAPTER SIX

LEFT BEHIND!

"Watch therefore: for ye know not what hour your Lord
doth come" (Matthew 24:42).

Nearly every newspaper I read has something in it related to
Bible prophecy. And I believe these are signs God has given to show
us how little time we have left before our world comes to an end.

Listen to these headlines from the *Daily News* here in Los
Angeles.

Bridges Falling Into Ruins. More than a quarter of the
nation's bridges are too weak, dilapidated or
overburdened for their current traffic according to
federal records that detail an American road system that
hasn't kept pace... (ibid., February 20, 2001, p. 1).

America is the greatest nation on earth, but we can't
even keep our roads and bridges operating! When we
see the fluctuations of the stock market, and the
growing energy crisis, it causes many people to wonder
how long America can go on.

Drug Deficit Hits Hospitals. Hospitals nationwide are
rationing adult tetanus shots...because of a huge
shortage of the crucial vaccine. It's one of the worst
drug shortages facing hospitals in years – and don't
expect it to be the last. Shortages of medications that
hospitals use every day are (now) occurring with more
frequency, and worse, they more often involve products
with few good alternatives...(it) haunts doctors and
pharmacists struggling to cope... Hospitals are feeling
shortages sooner than ever before because, faced with
steep medical costs, most now keep only a few days'
supply in inventory (ibid., pp. 1, 6).

Two doctors in our church confirm this report. Most
hospitals are no longer completely safe.

Kilimanjaro Ice Field Melting. The white ice atop Africa's Mount Kilimanjaro...could be disappearing, the victim of a process shrinking mountain glaciers everywhere. Lonnie G. Thompson, an Ohio State University researcher [said], "The ice will be gone by 2015 or so" (ibid., p. 7).

This is part of a dangerous world-wide ecological nightmare called "global warming" that threatens the environment today.

Sylmar Earthquake – Legacy of Fear Left by Temblor. Unpredictable disaster looms over their everyday life. Nurse Gloria Muetzel (says) "After the '94 earthquake I said, That's it. I'm out of here"...But even in Wisconsin, "it's always on your mind" (***Daily News***, February 9, 2001, pp. 1, 13).

We are warned of earthquakes and freak weather on national news programs nearly every day.

Car Bomb Explodes in Jerusalem. A car bomb exploded Thursday in a strictly Orthodox Jewish neighborhood in Jerusalem, shaking buildings and sending chunks of metal hurtling through the air...The bombing came two days after the rightist leader Ariel Sharon swept to a landslide victory in the vote for prime minister on a promise of restoring security (ibid., p. 19).

We hear about turmoil in the Middle East constantly now.

These may seem like random events. But those who know about Bible prophecy realize they are signs that we are now living in the last days. The thought of fulfilled prophecy flashes through my mind nearly every time I watch the news on television or read a secular newspaper. Events appear to be moving rapidly in the direction prophesied by the Bible centuries ago. Jesus said:

> "Watch therefore: for ye know not what hour your Lord doth come" (Matthew 24:42).

46

The Bible teaches that Christ is coming to meet true believers in the air. Some who don't believe the Bible mock at this miraculous event. They say that it will never happen. ***But they are wrong.*** One day soon the rapture will occur. ***And they will be left behind!***

The Conditions Before the Rapture

The Bible tells us exactly what the world will be like before the rapture:

> "But as the days of Noe (Noah) were, so shall also the coming of the Son of man be. For as in the days that were before the flood they were eating and drinking, marrying and giving in marriage, until the day that Noe (Noah) entered into the ark, And knew not until the flood came, and took them all away; so shall also the coming of the Son of man be" (Matthew 24:37-39).

Noah was a preacher of righteousness (II Peter 2:5). He warned his generation that judgment was coming. But people laughed at him and made fun of his message. They did not listen. They went right on with their sinful lives.

That's the way it is today. Someone invites you to church. You hear the sermon. Then you go right back to your old way of living. You don't repent. You don't fully place your trust in Jesus Christ. You go to church a time or two and then you stop attending.

You want to have "fun." To use Dr. A. W. Tozer's memorable phrase, you think the world is "a playground instead of a battleground." You think of life as a sort of nightclub. You feel that the whole purpose of life is to have "fun." You refuse to make time for God in a good church every Sunday. When any little thing comes up, you miss.

I say that you are not converted, that you are not a real Christian. When death comes for you, you will not be ready. ***When the rapture comes, you will be left on earth!***

> "Watch therefore: for ye know not what hour your Lord doth come" (Matthew 24:42).

The Danger of Being Unprepared for the Rapture

Some Bible teachers say that the virgins in Matthew 25:1-13 are the Jews in the Tribulation. But I question this interpretation. No one interpreted this passage that way until quite recently in church history. The old preachers said that the virgins in these verses referred to people who are unprepared to meet Christ. And I am convinced that the old-time preachers were right.

Jesus gave us this parable to illustrate a great spiritual truth. What *was* the great truth He was trying to get across? In Matthew 25:13 He tells us,

> "Watch therefore, for *ye* (not the Jews in the Tribulation,
> but "*you*") know neither the day nor the hour wherein
> the Son of man cometh" (Matthew 25:13).

So, this passage of Scripture is a warning to *you!*

Five of these virgins were wise. They were ready for the coming of Christ. But the other five were foolish. They were not ready. It is misleading to go into much detail when interpreting a parable. The simple message is this: ***many people will not be ready when the rapture occurs.***

> "And while they went to buy, the bridegroom came: and
> they that were ready went in with him to the marriage:
> ***and the door was shut"*** (Matthew 25:10).

After true Christians are raptured the door will be closed, just as the door of Noah's Ark was shut. ***No more people will get in.***

> "Afterward came also the other virgins, saying, Lord,
> Lord, open to us. But he answered and said, Verily I
> say unto you, I know you not" (Matthew 25:11-12).

Then Jesus makes this application to *you:*

> "Watch therefore, for *ye* know neither the day nor the
> hour wherein the Son of man cometh" (Matthew
> 25:13).

We can know the general period of time, but not the day or the hour. When that day and hour finally does come, it will be too late for you.

Many of Those Left Behind at the Rapture Will Be Given Up By God Because They Have Committed the Unpardonable Sin

In Revelation, chapter sixteen we learn that the wrath of God will be poured out on Christ-rejecting mankind in the second half of the Tribulation. Verse two tells us they will have painful sores. Verse four tells us the world's water supply will be poisoned. Verse eight tells us that mankind will be scorched with fire. Verse ten tells us that there will be great darkness and that people will gnaw on their tongues for pain. Verse eighteen tells us there will be a great, devastating earthquake. Verse twenty-one tells us that there will be "great hail," probably meteorites falling from the sky.

Will people turn to Christ when all this happens? *NO! They will not repent!* The passage tells us:

> "They repented not to give him glory" (Revelation 16:9).

Verse eleven says:

> "And blasphemed the God of heaven because of their pains and their sores, and repented not of their deeds" (Revelation 16:11).

The end of verse twenty-one tells us:

> "Men blasphemed God because of the plague of the hail; for the plague thereof was exceeding great" (Revelation 16:21).

You see, they will have been given up by God. The great revival described in Revelation 7:4-14 will be over. It will be too late for them to get saved. They will have committed the unpardonable sin.

> "God also gave them up" (Romans 1:24).

> "God gave them up" (Romans 1:26).

"God gave them over to a reprobate mind" (Romans 1:28).

Multitudes will be converted earlier in the Tribulation (Revelation 7:4-14). But they will be martyred for their faith (Revelation 13:7; 20:4). Then, toward the end of the Tribulation, a time will come when no one else is saved (Revelation 16:9, 11, 21). Mankind will be given up by God (cf. Romans 1:24, 26, 28). That's why you need to be converted now, so you will not have to go through any of this!

If you want to be raptured, *you need to get saved now, while God is still calling you.* Don't wait until God gives up on you.

Christ died to pay for your sins. He rose from the dead and is seated in Heaven at the right hand of God. Come to Him now and His Blood will wash your sins away. Then you'll be ready for the rapture. But if you wait, it will be said of you, "The Son has come, and you've been left behind."

> Life was filled with guns and war,
> And everyone got trampled on the floor.
> I wish we'd all been ready.
> Children died, the days grew cold,
> A piece of bread could buy a bag of gold.
> I wish we'd all been ready.
>
> Man and wife asleep in bed,
> She hears a noise and turns her head – he's gone.
> I wish we'd all been ready.
> Two men walking up a hill,
> One disappears and one's left standing still.
> I wish we'd all been ready.
>
> There's no time to change your mind,
> How could you have been so blind?
> The Father spoke, the demons dined,
> The Son has come, and you've been left behind.
> You've been left behind, you've been left behind.
> ("I Wish We'd All Been Ready" by Larry Norman, 1969).

CHAPTER SEVEN

THE "CHURCH" THAT WILL BE
LEFT BEHIND

"I will spue thee out of my mouth. Because thou sayest,
I am rich, and increased with goods, and have need of
nothing; and knowest not that thou art wretched, and
miserable, and poor, and blind, and naked" (Revelation
3:16-17).

A shocking number of churches will go right on as they are now
after the rapture. Many ministers will continue preaching – some of
them on national television. At first, people will think that the
rapture couldn't have happened at all. Then the Antichrist will be
unveiled. "That man of sin (will) be revealed, the son of perdition"
(II Thessalonians 2:3). Only at that time will many church members
realize that they have been left behind. At that time many will be
awakened and converted.

Yes, whole churches will be left behind at the rapture. In this
chapter I will deal with the false "church" that will be left behind in
the Tribulation.

The Identity of the "Church" That Will be Left Behind

II Timothy 3:1-13 gives the clearest description in the Bible of
the false "church" in the last days:

"This know also, that in the last days perilous times shall
come. For men shall be lovers of their own selves,
covetous, boasters, proud, blasphemers, disobedient to
parents, unthankful, unholy, Without natural affection,
trucebreakers, false accusers, incontinent, fierce,
despisers of those that are good, Traitors, heady,
highminded, lovers of pleasures more than lovers of
God; Having a form of godliness, but denying the power
thereof: from such turn away. For of this sort are they
which creep into houses, and lead captive silly women

laden with sins, led away with divers lusts, Ever learning, and never able to come to the knowledge of the truth. Now as Jannes and Jambres withstood Moses, so do these also resist the truth: men of corrupt minds, reprobate concerning the faith. But they shall proceed no further: for their folly shall be manifest unto all men, as theirs also was...Yea, and all that will live godly in Christ Jesus shall suffer persecution. But evil men and seducers shall wax worse and worse, deceiving, and being deceived" (II Timothy 3:1-13).

First, the "church" that will be left behind is going to be made up of people with unconverted hearts. They are described in II Timothy 3:5 as

"Having a form of godliness, but denying the power thereof: from such turn away" (II Timothy 3:5).

They will have "a form of godliness, but deny the power thereof." Galatians 5:19-21 also gives a description of people like this:

"Now the works of the flesh are manifest, which are these; Adultery, fornication, uncleanness, lasciviousness, Idolatry, witchcraft, hatred, variance, emulations, wrath, strife, seditions, heresies, Envyings, murders, drunkenness, revellings, and such like: of the which I tell you before, as I have also told you in time past, that *they which do such things shall not inherit the kingdom of God*" (Galatians 5:19-21).

If those verses describe you it indicates that you will be left at the rapture. You "shall not inherit the kingdom of God."

We are told in II Corinthians 5:17,

"If any man be in Christ, he is a new creature: old things are passed away; behold, all things are become new" (II Corinthians 5:17).

When people are truly converted there is a new direction in their lives. The converted person loves things that he disliked before, and hates things he once loved.

A person who doesn't *love* being in a good church at every opportunity has never been converted. A person who doesn't hate his old way of loose living has never been converted. After the rapture, people who love to sin and live loose lives will suddenly realize what fools they have been. How about you?

Second, the "church" that is left behind will be made up of people who resist the truth.

> "Now as Jannes and Jambres withstood Moses, so do
> these also resist the truth: men of corrupt minds,
> reprobate concerning the faith" (II Timothy 3:8).

Jannes and Jambres were the two Egyptian magicians who were against Moses in Pharaoh's court, in Egypt. These men would not listen to Moses and they rejected God. People in the church that will be left behind are just like them, "So do these also resist the truth" (II Timothy 3:8).

Do you "resist the truth" that you need Jesus Christ to save you? Do you "resist the truth" that you need to have your sins cleansed by the Blood of Christ? Do you "resist the truth" that you need to be converted and come into a local church? If you "resist" these great Bible truths you are no more saved than those two wicked Egyptian magicians in Pharaoh's palace long ago. You are part of the false "church" that will not be raptured.

Third, the false "church" will become increasingly worse as the age draws to a close:

> "But evil men and seducers shall wax (i.e. grow) worse
> and worse, deceiving, and being deceived" (II Timothy
> 3:13).

We now see so-called "Christians" doing things, and believing things, that no one thought a real Christian could do or believe when I was a little boy a half-century ago. Older Christians I talk to are constantly shocked and dismayed by what they see people doing who claim to be saved today. And the Bible tells us that it will get "worse and worse" as the rapture draws near (II Timothy 3:13). These people may think they are saved, but they are actually part of the false "church" that will be left on earth. What about you?

Fourth, the "church" that will be left behind does not put up with sound doctrine:

> "Preach the word; be instant in season, out of season; ***reprove, rebuke, exhort*** with all longsuffering and doctrine. ***For the time will come when they will not endure sound doctrine;*** but after their own lusts shall they heap to themselves teachers, having itching ears; And they shall turn away their ears from the truth, and shall be turned unto fables" (II Timothy 4:2-4).

People who are part of the false "church" don't want to hear preaching that contains reproof, rebuking and exhortation (II Timothy 4:2). They have "itching ears" (verse 3). They want to have their ears tickled with "positive thinking," pop-psychology, or novel ideas – even novel ideas about Bible prophecy. They don't want to hear old-fashioned ***preaching***, like I remember from fifty years ago!

How about you? If you want a smiling preacher with a "positive" message, to make you feel better, I think you will be part of the false "church" that will be left on earth.

Fifth, the "church" that is left behind will have its folly manifested to everyone:

> "But they shall proceed no further: for their folly shall be manifest unto all men..." (II Timothy 3:9).

The word "folly" here means "madness" according to ***Strong's Concordance.***

Many of the things so-called "Christians" practice in their "churches" are absolute ***madness!*** They will tell you that it's all "up to date," modern, and successful. But it is really insanity.

Christ says,

> "Because thou art lukewarm, and neither cold nor hot, I will spue thee out of my mouth" (Revelation 3:16).

He will spit the false "church" out of His mouth because of the "madness" of lukewarm "Christianity" in the last days.

The folly and insanity of the false "church" will be seen by all, because it will be left behind at the rapture. How about you? Will the madness of your life show that you are not a real Christian in that day?

The Awakening and Conversion of Many in the False "Church" That Will Be Left at the Rapture

The parable of the Wise and Foolish Virgins is recorded in Matthew 25:1-13. As we showed in Chapter One, Arno C. Gaebelein, Wilbur M. Smith, James O. Combs, and other Bible scholars teach that these verses refer to Christians in this age. I am convinced that they are correct, and that this parable refers to the rapture and what will happen directly afterwards:

> "And while they went to buy, the bridegroom came; and they that were ready went in with him to the marriage: and the door was shut. Afterward came also the other virgins, saying, Lord, Lord, open to us. But he answered and said, Verily I say unto you, I know you not" (Matthew 25:10-12).

Those who are truly converted "went in with him (Christ) to the marriage." That means they are caught up to meet the Lord in the air (cf. I Thessalonians 4:16-17). After the rapture, the false "Christians" (the foolish virgins) say to Christ, "Lord, Lord, open to us." They realize that they have been left behind. But Christ replies, "Verily I say unto you, I know you not."

I believe strongly, with Dr. Wilbur M. Smith and the other scholars I have mentioned, that this is the way *you* will feel when you realize that you have missed the rapture. It will terrify you, and some of you will then begin to seek Christ earnestly for the first time in your life.

> "And ye shall seek me, and find me, when ye shall search for me with all your heart" (Jeremiah 29:13).

When you search for Christ with all your heart you will find Him – even in the early part of the Tribulation period.

In Revelation 7:4-14 we read about 144,000 Jewish people and "a great multitude, which no man could number" of Gentiles who will be converted in a short period of time at the beginning of the

Tribulation. This will be the third of the greatest revivals in history, and the most gigantic one of all.

Between about 30 AD and 96 AD the first great revival swept hundreds of thousands of people into salvation. This revival began on the day of Pentecost (Acts 2:1-47) and continued for about sixty-five years.

The second of the greatest revivals of history was the Reformation. Beginning with Luther's posting of the Ninety-Five Theses on the church door at Wittenberg in 1517, and continuing through the death of John Calvin in 1564, the Reformation was supremely a revival:

> The Reformation was a great and general revival of religion during which tens of thousands of souls were born again. This gracious spiritual awakening profoundly affected Germany, Switzerland, France, Holland, and Great Britain; also to a considerable degree Spain and Italy. The saving truths of the Word of God became so widespread and deeply rooted in the hearts of the people, that the Church of Rome tried in vain to halt its progress by kindling the fires of persecution. ***Without doubt the Protestant Reformation in the sixteenth century was the greatest revival of religion that the church witnessed since the days of the Apostles*** (Gilbert Egerton, *Flame of God*, Ambassador Publications, Belfast, Northern Ireland, 1987, p. 30).

The third of the greatest revivals in history will be the one in the Tribulation period, recorded in Revelation 7:4-14,

> "These are they which came out of great tribulation, and have washed their robes, and made them white in the blood of the Lamb" (Revelation 7:14).

The revival of the first century lasted about sixty years. It took Christianity from a tiny group of converted Jews to a world-wide religion. The Reformation revival lasted about forty-seven years. It spread genuine Christian conversion throughout the world. The third and greatest revival of all time, in the Tribulation period, will sweep thousands of Jews and millions of Gentiles into the Kingdom of God.

The first of these revivals lasted about sixty-six years (AD 30 to AD 96). The second one was about forty-seven years long (AD 1517 to AD 1564). The third one will happen during the first part of the seven-year Tribulation. It will be shorter in length, probably because of mass movement and communication made possible by technology in the modern world.

But before you get too ecstatic and joyful, remember that each of these revivals takes place during great persecution. In the first century, the Emperor Nero executed both the Apostle Peter and the Apostle Paul, plus thousands of others – merely because they were Christians. At the end of this revival the Emperor Domitian once again harassed and murdered Christians. Historian Earle E. Cairns writes:

> Nero had the dubious distinction of being the first major persecutor of the Christian Church. Tacitus recorded the rumor that Nero had ordered the fire that destroyed part of the city of Rome. This rumor was so widespread that Nero had to find a scapegoat. He diverted feelings against himself to the Christians by accusing them of arson and by engaging in (the) destruction of the Christians. Peter and Paul died in this period.
>
> Persecution broke out again in 95 (AD) during the reign of the despotic Domitian. The Jews had refused to pay a poll tax that had been levied for the support of Capitolinus Jupiter (an idol). Because the Christians continued to be associated with the Jews, they also suffered the effects of the emperor's wrath. It was during this persecution that the Apostle John was exiled to the Isle of Patmos, where he wrote the Book of Revelation (Earle E. Cairns, ***Christianity Through the Centuries***, Zondervan, 1981, p. 91).

During the Reformation revival, horrible persecution against true Christians was also wide spread. Dr. Cairns writes:

> The Roman church had two weapons of coercion to back up the propaganda of the Jesuits. These were the Inquisition and the Index. The...Roman Inquisition was proclaimed by a Papal bull of Paul III in 1542 as

an instrument to deal with heresy anywhere until it was abolished in 1854. Those accused were always presumed guilty till they proved their innocence; they were never confronted with their accusers; they could be made to testify against themselves; and they could be tortured to extract a confession. If sentenced, they were punished by loss of property, imprisonment, or burning at the stake, unless they confessed and recanted. These punishments were carried out by the secular authorities under the watchful eye of the inquisitors (Earle E. Cairns, op. cit., p. 348).

During the Reformation revival thousands of people were executed for their faith in Jesus Christ. Virtually every Protestant in France was murdered on St. Bartholomew's Day in 1572, in one great bloody slaughter.

Before you decide to wait until after the rapture to be converted, remember that it will cost *you* persecution and execution, just as it did the Christians of the first century and the sixteenth century. Here's what will happen in the Tribulation:

"And they (the unsaved world) worshipped the dragon (Satan) which gave power unto the beast: and they worshipped the beast (the Antichrist), saying, Who is like unto the beast? who is able to make war with him? And there was given unto him a mouth speaking great things and blasphemies; and power was given unto him to continue forty and two months. And he opened his mouth in blasphemy against God, to blaspheme his name, and his tabernacle, and them that dwell in heaven. *And it was given unto him to make war with the saints, and to overcome them:* and power was given him over all kindreds, and tongues, and nations. And all that dwell upon the earth shall worship him, whose names are not written in the book of life of the Lamb slain from the foundation of the world. If any man have an ear, let him hear" (Revelation 13:4-9).

The "beast" is the Antichrist, the coming world-ruler. The "forty and two months" is the last three-and-a-half years of the Tribulation.

"And it was given unto him to make war with the saints, and to overcome them" (Revelation 13:7).

The Antichrist will destroy virtually every Christian who is saved in the Tribulation revival.

> "And I saw the souls of them that were beheaded for the witness of Jesus, and for the word of God, and which had not worshipped the beast (the Antichrist), neither his image…" (Revelation 20:4).

Remember that the French used the guillotine during their revolution until the streets of Paris ran red with the blood of those who were beheaded. This will happen again, to those who become Christians during the Tribulation.

During the period known as the "Dark Ages" or "Middle Ages," millions of true Christians were burned at the stake or horribly tortured in other ways for their faith. Dr. J. M. Carroll said:

> These Christians were the perpetual objects of bitter and relentless persecution. History shows that during the period of the "Dark Ages"…*there were about fifty million of these Christians who died martyrs' deaths* (J. M. Carroll, *The Trail of Blood*, published by Ashland Avenue Baptist Church, Lexington, Kentucky, 1931, p. 54).

This will happen again to those who are converted in the Tribulation revival.

I would not wait to be saved until after the rapture if I were you. I would seek Christ now, while it is so much easier.

> In times like these, you need a Saviour,
> In times like these, you need an anchor.
> Be very sure, be very sure
> Your anchor holds and grips the Solid Rock.
>
> This Rock is Jesus, yes, He's the One;
> This Rock is Jesus, the only One!
> Be very sure, be very sure,
> Your anchor holds and grips the Solid Rock!
>   ("In Times Like These" by Ruth Caye Jones, 1944).

CHAPTER EIGHT

REVIVAL AMID APOSTASY AND PERSECUTION

> "These are they which came out of great tribulation, and have washed their robes, and made them white in the blood of the lamb" (Revelation 7:14).

Jesus told us to beware of setting an exact time for the rapture:

> "But of that day and hour knoweth no man, no, not the angels of heaven, but my Father only" (Matthew 24:36).

But He also told us that we could know the general time of the end:

> "But as the days of Noe (Noah) were, so shall also the coming of the Son of man be. For as in the days that were before the flood they were eating and drinking, marrying and giving in marriage, until the day that Noe (Noah) entered into the ark, And knew not until the flood came, and took them all away; so shall also the coming of the Son of man be" (Matthew 24:37-39).

That's the way people are right now, today. They are living just the way people lived in the time of Noah, recorded in Genesis, chapters four through seven. In Noah's day, multitudes had called on the name of the Lord (Genesis 4:26). But these so-called "believers" never entered the Ark of salvation.

> "And the Lord said unto Noah, Come thou and all thy house into the ark; for thee have I seen righteous before me in this generation" (Genesis 7:1).

> "And Noah went in, and his sons, and his wife, and his sons' wives with him, into the ark" (Genesis 7:7).

> "And all flesh died that moved upon the earth...All in whose nostrils was the breath of life, of all that was in

> the dry land died...and Noah only remained alive, and
> they that were with him in the ark" (Genesis 7:21-23).

> "(God) spared not the old world, but saved Noah the
> eighth person, a preacher of righteousness, bringing in
> the flood upon the world of the ungodly" (II Peter 2:5).

The so-called "godly line" of Seth was drowned in the Flood. They had called on the name of the Lord (Genesis 4:26), but they were judged by the Flood. And the Bible calls them "the ungodly" (II Peter 2:5). They were religious, but they were lost. The *Scofield Study Bible* says, "Noah, 'a preacher of righteousness,' (was) given 120 years, but he won no convert" (note on Genesis 6:4). The "religious" people of Noah's day were like millions of professing "Christians" today. They were not prepared for Judgment. How about *you?*

In Matthew 24:37-39, Jesus said that people would be caught unprepared for judgment in the last days, just as they were unprepared in Noah's time. He continued by saying:

> "Then shall two be in the field; the one shall be taken,
> and the other left. Two women shall be grinding at the
> mill; the one shall be taken, and the other left. Watch
> therefore: for ye know not what hour your Lord doth
> come" (Matthew 24:40-42).

I believe that this refers to the rapture of true Christians:

> "Behold, I shew you a mystery; We shall not all sleep,
> but we shall all be changed, In a moment, in the
> twinkling of an eye, at the last trump: for the trumpet
> shall sound, and the dead shall be raised incorruptible,
> and we shall be changed" (I Corinthians 15:51-52).

> "And the dead in Christ shall rise first: Then we which
> are alive and remain shall be caught up together with
> them in the clouds, to meet the Lord in the air..." (I
> Thessalonians 4:16-17).

When the Antichrist signs a treaty with Israel (Daniel 9:27), then the great Tribulation will begin, a time of judgment, as God sent judgment in Noah's day.

Where We Are Right Now

"Let no man deceive you by any means: for that day shall not come, except there come a falling away first, and that man of sin be revealed, the son of perdition" (II Thessalonians 2:3).

Dr. W. A. Criswell said of this verse:

The phrase "a falling away" may be translated "the apostasy." The use of the article [the] indicates that Paul has in mind a specific apostasy. The implication is that before "the day of the Lord" there will occur a marked falling away of professed believers (*The Criswell Study Bible*, note on II Thessalonians 2:3).

All signs indicate that we are living in that period today. We are *now* in the Great Apostasy. The "man of sin," the Antichrist, will be "revealed" in the future, during the Tribulation. But the "falling away" has been going on for well over a hundred years, since the days of Charles G. Finney. This man, Finney, and those who copied his methods, filled our churches with lost people who "called on the name of the Lord," as they did in the days of Noah, but were not truly saved by entering into the Ark of salvation (a type of Christ).

As a result of adopting Finney's methods of "decisionism," the churches became full of unconverted people. The great Protestant denominations went into apostasy because decisionism filled the church rolls with people who had never experienced salvation. *Liberalism did not cause the apostasy. The apostasy was caused by decisionism.* Liberalism was the *fruit* of decisionism, as I have shown in my book, *Today's Apostasy* (Hearthstone, 1999).

In our day, as Dr. A. W. Tozer said, "probably less than one out of ten evangelicals knows anything experientially about the new birth" (quoted in *Getting Evangelicals Saved*, Bethany House Publishers, 1989, p. 46).

That is the reason so many "Christians" miss church, live loose lives, and hold false doctrines. Decisionism has filled our churches with lost people who know nothing about the new birth. Millions of them cling to a false hope, but they are not *in* Christ. They are not *in* the ark of salvation.

What Will Happen Next

If A. W. Tozer's estimate is close to being correct, over ninety percent of those who think they are saved will be left behind at the rapture.

Jesus said:

> "But as the days of Noe (Noah) were, so shall also the coming of the Son of man be...(They) knew not until the flood came, and took them all away; so shall also the coming of the Son of man be. Then shall two be in the field; the one shall be taken, and the other left. Two women shall be grinding at the mill; the one shall be taken, and the other left. Watch therefore: for ye know not what hour your Lord doth come" (Matthew 24:37-42).

Then, in the following parable, Christ said:

> "And while they went to buy, the bridegroom came; and they that were ready went in with him to the marriage: and the door was shut" (Matthew 25:10).

I know that there are several theories about what this means. But they don't convince me. The plain statement of Scripture shows that many will *not be ready for the rapture!*

> "...the bridegroom (Jesus) came; and they that were ready went in with him to the marriage: and the door was shut" (Matthew 25:10).

What will happen then?

> "Afterward came also the other virgins saying, Lord, Lord, open to us. But he answered and said, Verily I say unto you, I know you not. Watch therefore, for ye know neither the day nor the hour wherein the Son of man cometh" (Matthew 25:11-13).

A Word of Warning to Those Who Disagree

Even if you disagree with my view of the above verses, you must admit (if you think about it) that many who believe they are saved will be left at the rapture because they are not truly converted. Logic, as well as Scripture, demands that this will happen. Jesus told us,

> "Not everyone that saith unto me, Lord, Lord, shall enter into the kingdom of heaven; but he that doeth the will of my Father which is in heaven. Many will say to me in that day, Lord, Lord, have we not prophesied in thy name? and in thy name have cast out devils? and in thy name done many wonderful works? And then will I profess unto them, I never knew you: depart from me, ye that work iniquity" (Matthew 7:21-23).

These verses are so clear that I don't see how anyone can disagree with our basic position: ***Many people who think they are saved will actually be unprepared for the rapture because they are not truly converted! How about you?*** As the old song put it,

> Oh, can we say we are ready, brother?
> Ready for the soul's bright home?
> Say, will He find you and me still watching,
> Waiting, waiting when the Lord shall come?
> ("Will Jesus Find Us Watching?"
> by Fanny J. Crosby, 1820-1915)

Many will ***not*** be ready for "the soul's bright home" when the rapture comes!

How Revival Will Come After the Rapture, Followed by Terrible Persecution

A great revival will be sent by God during the Tribulation, after true Christians are caught away. Dr. John R. Rice said:

> After every saved person shall be taken away with Jesus, and when the Antichrist himself will rule on the

earth, will come the Great Tribulation. The Antichrist will refuse people who do not take his mark the right to buy and sell. Those who get converted under these conditions will surely risk their lives for Christ. And yet, the Bible tells us plainly that in the Great Tribulation there will come the most marvelous revival...In the first part of this chapter (Revelation 7), we have a discussion of 144,000 Israelites who will be converted during this time of the Great Tribulation...But aside from the Israelites, here is "a great multitude, which no man could number, of all nations, and kindreds, and people, and tongues" who are saved. These will come out of the Great Tribulation... ***What a revival God will give in the tribulation time!*** (John R. Rice, ***We Can Have Revival Now***, Sword of the Lord, 1950, pp. 30-33).

We are told that 144,000 Jews will be saved in the Tribulation (Revelation 7:4-8). Then we are told that a "multitude, which no man could number," of all races on earth, will be truly converted in this remarkable revival (Revelation 7:9-17).

"And he said to me, These are they which came out of great tribulation, and have washed their robes, and made them white in the blood of the Lamb" (Revelation 7:14).

Remember, according to the figures given in Revelation 7:4-17, ***this will be the greatest revival in the history of Christianity.*** Millions will be truly converted in a few months, including tens of thousands of Jewish people!

How can it be? Of course, revival comes from God. But what human event could He use to awaken people from the sleep of death? I believe that God may well use the rapture itself to trigger this greatest-of-all revivals.

"Afterward came also the other virgins, saying, Lord, Lord, open to us. But he answered and said, Verily I say unto you, I know you not" (Matthew 25:11-12).

Imagine the horror that millions would experience when they realize that the rapture has come and they have been *shut out!* They would probably say words like this:

> "Lord, Lord, have we not prophesied (preached and witnessed) in thy name? and in thy name have cast out devils? and in thy name done many wonderful works?" (Matthew 7:22).

Great fear would then grip them as they viewed the events they knew would happen developing quickly in the world around them.

Millions know about these events from Hal Lindsey's best-seller, *The Late Great Planet Earth.* Millions more know about the Tribulation from Dr. Tim LaHaye's best-selling *Left Behind* books. Suddenly these people will be confronted with the horrible truth. They will quake and tremble, and cry out, "I'VE BEEN LEFT BEHIND!"

I believe that the horror of this knowledge will awaken literally millions of people to their lost condition. God will use it to arouse them from dead religion.

When *you* are left behind you will then see that you were never converted at all. You will realize that you made a "decision," but you never saw the depths of your sin and you never knew Christ in reality. *You will be horror-stricken, filled with bone-shaking terror!*

Oh, how I wish you would examine yourself *now!*

> "Examine yourselves, whether ye be in the faith" (II Corinthians 13:5).

If you did not come to the end of yourself in a real conversion, you are still lost. *If you rested in the fact that you merely "changed your way of living," you are still lost.* If you comforted yourself because you believed the facts of the gospel, *you are still as lost as the Devil*, who believes all of the "Roman Road" and the "plan of salvation." If you are trusting the fact that you made a decision or said a "sinner's prayer," you are still lost. If you think you are saved because you confessed sin or "asked Jesus into your heart," you are still lost!

66

Oh, I beg you to give up your false salvation! Don't be *left behind* at the rapture! Don't go to Hell when you die! Give up your false conversion, and seek Jesus Christ, the Son of God, the Second Person of the Trinity, the Messiah, the Deliverer, the mediator between God and man! Seek Jesus until you find Him and are washed from your sins by His Blood!

> "It is time to seek the Lord, till he come and rain righteousness upon you" (Hosea 10:12).

> "Christ Jesus, whom God hath set forth to be a propitiation through faith in his blood" (Romans 3:24-25).

But, someone says, "I can wait and be saved later, in the Great Tribulation." Ah, what a clever deceiver the Devil is! True, you *may* be saved later, but think of the horror you will have to go through! It will be even worse than the terrible persecution people are experiencing in China and Viet Nam today when they become true Christians. They are having revival amid great persecution right now. It will be even worse then, in the Tribulation.

The Antichrist will "overcome" real believers during this period (Revelation 13:7). The government will behead many for "the witness of Jesus" (Revelation 20:4). Those who become Christians in that time will be "slain for the word of God, and for the testimony which they held" (Revelation 6:9).

Do not wait! Do not be left behind! Do not tarry until you are tortured, imprisoned and beheaded if you become a Christian! Turn to Jesus Christ *fully* – now!

CHAPTER NINE

SUICIDE IN THE TRIBULATION

"And in those days shall men seek death" (Revelation 9:6).

The Bible tells us that some demons are now in Hell:

"God spared not the angels that sinned, but cast them down to hell, and delivered them into chains of darkness, to be reserved unto judgment" (II Peter 2:4).

But other demons are not in Hell. They are loose on the earth. Jesus confronted a man who was possessed with many of these "loose" demons, an event recorded in Luke 8:26-39.

"And Jesus asked him, saying, What is thy name? And he said, Legion: because many devils were entered into him. And they besought him that he would not command them to go out into the deep"
(Luke 8:30-31).

These demons did not want to be cast into "the deep." This appears to be the place spoken of in II Peter 2:4, where other demons are already in "chains of darkness." So, there are demons loose on earth now, and there are other demons bound in "chains of darkness."

In the Tribulation period, demons which are bound in Hell today will be released, as a judgment, to torment sinful men on earth. This is prophesied in Revelation 9:1-12,

"And the fifth angel sounded, and I saw a star fall from heaven unto the earth: and to him was given the key of the bottomless pit. And he opened the bottomless pit; and there arose a smoke out of the pit, as the smoke of a great furnace; and the sun and the air were darkened by reason of the smoke of the pit. And there came out of the smoke locusts upon the earth: and unto them was given power, as the scorpions of the earth have power. And it was commanded them that they should not hurt the grass of the earth, neither any green thing, neither any tree; but only those men which have not the seal of God in their foreheads. And to them it was given that they should not kill them, but that they should be tormented five months: and their torment was as the torment of a scorpion, when he striketh a man. And in those days shall men seek death, and shall not find it; and shall desire to die, and death shall flee from them. And the shapes of the locusts were like unto horses prepared unto battle; and on their heads were as it were crowns like gold, and their faces were as the faces of men. And they had hair as the hair of women, and their teeth were as the teeth of lions. And they had breastplates, as it were breastplates of iron; and the sound of their wings was as the sound of chariots of many horses running to battle. And they had tails like unto scorpions, and there were stings in their tails: and their power was to hurt men five months. And they had a king over them, which is the angel of the bottomless pit, whose name in the Hebrew tongue is Abaddon, but in the Greek tongue hath his name Apollyon. One woe is past; and, behold, there come two woes more hereafter" (Revelation 9:1-12).

What a horrible picture of the future this is! In this passage of Scripture we are told that the "bottomless pit" will be opened, and demons which were formerly chained up will be loosed on the earth.

Dr. John R. Rice said concerning this passage:

We do not doubt that the "locusts" (because locusts are a destructive plague) are here demons. There was a literal plague of locusts in Egypt that ate up the crops, but these are not literal insects. They are released out of the pit of Hell. The message is spiritual and these locusts eat not the grass, the trees, or any green thing, but come to torture only "those men which have not the seal of God in their foreheads."

Tortured and tormented by these "locusts," these demons from Hell, "...in those days shall men seek death, and shall not find it; and shall desire to die, and death shall flee from them" (Revelation 9:6).

I think the torment mentioned here is spiritual torment with a troubled, agonized mind. Here is something like that that came to Judas when he said, "I have betrayed innocent blood" (Matthew 27:4) and went and hanged himself.

The picture of these locusts is fantastic, like a terrible dream, like a summing up of all the fears and troubles and heartbreaks of men put in poetic language. For "their teeth were as the teeth of lions" (v. 8), but they do not tear the bodies of men; rather, they torment the soul. Their "tails like unto scorpions" (v. 10) hurt men, but their hurt is not simply or only physical pain but torment of soul.

The "king over them" (v. 11) is that fallen angel or archangel "of the bottomless pit, whose name in the Hebrew tongue is Abaddon, but in the Greek tongue his name is Apollyon." Both mean "the destroyer." You will note that this trouble is for unsaved men. "Those which have not the seal of God in their foreheads" (v. 4). And they (the demons) do not kill lost people but torment them (v. 5). ***Can you imagine the awful ruin of soul when men are turned over to evil spirits?*** (John R. Rice, ***Behold, He Cometh! – A Commentary on Revelation***, Sword of the Lord, 1977, pp. 169-171).

Great psychological torment, brought on by increased demonic activity, will occur during the final years of the Tribulation period.

I have seen such judgment come to lost people even now, before the Tribulation. One woman I knew bitterly refused to hear the gospel for years. She spoke viciously against church attendance and insisted that she could worship "her god" in the yard, doing gardening work on Sunday morning instead of attending preaching services at church.

Then her mind began to go and she became severely depressed. She tried to commit suicide by driving her car into a lake. They dragged her out of the water and pumped out her lungs. She was more tormented than ever. She literally sought "death and (did) not find it" (Revelation 9:6). They put her on medication, but it did not seem to help. Thoughts of suicide filled her mind constantly.

My wife begged her to be converted. But she insisted that she was already a Christian. She said that she worshipped "god" in her own way, while doing work in her yard on Sundays.

One day her mind snapped completely. She drank a glass of liquor followed by a large glass of green weed poison. She went out to her garage to die. They found her out there, crawling in a poisoned stupor in a circle on the floor of the garage. We were told that she had been groveling around like that for over twelve hours. She died in the hospital.

They called me to conduct her funeral. I could smell the ghastly scent of the weed poison seeping out of the edges of her sealed coffin. It was a hideous reminder of the terrible judgments that await those who reject Biblical conversion in the Tribulation:

> "And in those days shall men seek death, and shall not
> find it; and shall desire to die, and death shall flee from
> them" (Revelation 9:6).

Suicide Today

An average of 75 Americans take their own lives by suicide every day. Suicide is the 10th leading cause of death in this country. The largest number of those who commit suicide are young people under the age of thirty. Suicide is the third leading cause of death among those between the ages of 15 and 19 years old. Suicide is the second leading cause of death among college students ages 20 to 25 years old. More than 35,000 people take their own lives every year in America. The world-wide figure for suicides is 1/2 million people every year. Over one thousand people in the world commit suicide each day, with ten times that number attempting it without success.

Factors most commonly associated with suicide are death of a loved one, loneliness and social isolation, chronic illness, psychological disturbances, alcoholism and drugs. The highest suicide rates occur among doctors, psychiatrists and dentists, higher than any other occupations. Think of it! Doctors, psychiatrists and other health-givers are among the highest groups who commit suicide! Many of them can't help *themselves!* How can they help *you?* In case you hadn't noticed, things are out of control!

71

Sweden, like the United States, has a high standard of living and a highly industrialized society. This small country already has what many American liberals say is their goal for us in the United States.

Poverty and unemployment are almost unknown in Sweden. Medical care is socialized. It is "free" for everyone. Government pensions are given from the cradle to the grave. Swedish parents are given a grant of money at birth for each child, plus an annual allowance.

Sweden's "sex freedom" is known the world over. Eighty to ninety percent of their young people have had sexual experiences before marriage. There is little sexual repression of any kind.

Yet Sweden has the fourth largest number of suicides – higher than any other Western nation. A larger percentage of their people – and a far larger percentage of Swedish women – commit suicide than do Americans.

However, in Sweden, church attendance is at an all-time low. Less than 8 percent attend church regularly. *That's the reason!* You can have lots of money, and lots of health care, and lots of sex – *but if you don't have God and the local church, you don't really have anything worth living for! That's why you need be in a Bible-believing church next Sunday!* You need God. You need to be forgiven by Christ. You need to be in church every time the door is open!

Think of it. Suicide is the number two killer of college-age young people! Many young people who never actually kill themselves have considered doing it. Psychiatrists tell us that most people in all age groups have at least thought about it. So it's worth taking a few minutes to find out what the Bible says about suicide.

People Commit Suicide Because They Have Come to Hate Life

Depression is one of the leading reasons for suicide. One man in the Bible became so depressed that he said,

> "(I) choose strangling and death rather than my life.
> I loathe it" (I hate life) (Job 7:15-16).

Although Job became very depressed, he did not commit suicide because he knew God.

Someone may say, "This message doesn't apply to me. I'm not going to commit suicide." One man from the Philippines said, "Dr. Hymers' sermons don't apply to me. I went to Catholic school. Don't worry about me. My family is religious. I'm OK." But Jesus said, "Ye must be born again" (John 3:7). He said, "Except a man be born again, he cannot see the kingdom of God" (John 3:3). This chapter *does* apply to you, whoever you are. Depression and thoughts of suicide could come flooding into your mind some day soon as a result of unforeseen events in your future.

Many people who won't ever commit suicide *will* become depressed. People tell me all the time that they feel lonely and despondent. You wonder if you can make it in life. You wonder if you'll ever have a normal home. You wonder if you'll be a success. And you're afraid that happiness will elude you. You're often afraid that you'll never be completely happy or fulfilled.

And most people are lonely. There's an empty, hollow, aching spot in your heart – even when you're in a crowd.

I was talking to a young man I know the other day. He's about 20 or 21 years old. I overheard him say this to another person, "I went to a night club in downtown LA. I danced with those Spanish girls until 4:00 AM. I didn't get to bed until 5:00 AM, and I came to work at 8:00 – but I don't feel too bad." I thought, "You can do that when you're twenty. But wait a few years!" That kind of partying will sap away the strength of your youth and you'll be old before your time. You can't live a wild life like that without it ruining your body and destroying your soul.

But there are so many people like him. Why does he go dancing all night? He's lonely and depressed. He's looking for excitement. I know an older man here in Los Angeles who sits by the hour in a coffee shop so he won't have to go back to his empty room.

Most of you are like those people. You're lonely – even with all our leisure time and our alcohol and our entertainment and our drugs – none of it has taken away your emptiness and loneliness. Many people tell me that their city is one of the most lonely places on earth.

You may go to the dance hall like that boy. You may sit staring at the wall in a bar. Everyone is jumping to the music. The lights are flashing on and off and the rhythm is pounding. The room is jammed with the bodies of pulsating people. But somehow you're still alone – even in that crowd of people. *Alone in the crowd!*

How many lonely people are there in your city? Are you one of them? Are you searching for a real friend? Are you looking for someone who will understand you and care about you?

That is why you need to be in a good church – every time the door is open! Make the church your second home. Let the people in the church become your new family. Let the preacher become your friend, and the people in church your new brothers and sisters. You'll find Christ there. You'll find love there. In a good church, the people will be the best family and the best friends you've ever had. Come into the family of God, the local church.

There's no need for you to live a barren, depressed, lonely and meaningless life. ***Come to Christ and come into a good church. There's a better way to live!***

People will often try to stop you from coming to Christ. They are afraid that you may become a zealous Christian. Parents and friends will often try to stop you from coming to church. Many who call themselves "Christians" will try to stop you from coming, especially if you're getting serious about religion.

One young man was driving without a license. He got a ticket on Thursday. His "Christian" family (who were supposedly saved in 1998) said to him, "Stop going to that Baptist church. You wouldn't have gotten a ticket if you had been driving on Sunday like you were supposed to." These people actually thought that if he had missed church and been driving on Sunday he wouldn't have gotten a ticket! They tried their best to keep him from going to church, which they blamed for the ticket. My question is this, "Don't they give tickets on Sunday?" They will often say almost anything to keep you from being in a good church, even something as ridiculous as that.

Yes, great numbers of people become so lonely that they go into deep depression – and many even commit suicide – because they don't have Christ. They don't have the hope and peace that only Christ can give. They come to the place where they actually hate life. They hate the way they feel much of the time.

People Attempt Suicide For Two Main Reasons

1. Either it's a cry for help
2. Or it's an attempt to escape.

Many people who attempt suicide don't really mean to kill themselves. They are *really* crying for help. They're saying, "I can't make it! I'm hurting! Please, somebody, help me!" They are signaling for help through an attempted suicide.

But suicide is the wrong way to cry for help. You might slip up and *really* kill yourself! And suicide is horrible. It's often an attempt to escape from the great problems and sins of life.

Suicide isn't the only way people try to escape from their problems and sins. Many people block their minds out with drugs or alcohol in an attempt to escape from the reality of a meaningless life. Others use sex or cheap thrills of one sort or another to feel better – to forget their boredom and their lonely, loveless existence.

They call it "escapism." That's why so many people watch endless television or play video games by the hour. That's why they gamble. They want to escape from a life of boredom.

But the Bible asks this question:

"How shall we escape, if we neglect so great salvation?" (Hebrews 2:3).

God sent Jesus Christ to die on the Cross to pay for your sins. The Blood of Christ can wash your sins away if you will come to Him and be converted. Christ did not stay in the grave. He rose from the dead, literally and physically, on the third day after He was buried. And Christ ascended into Heaven. He arose into another dimension. And the Bible teaches that He is alive in the heavenlies right now. And you can come to Christ. He will forgive you and save you and convert you. Jesus Christ can give you hope and forgiveness. *That is the great salvation which God has prepared for you.*

But what if you *neglect* that salvation? "How shall we escape, if we neglect so great salvation?" That's what Saul did. Saul neglected God. He turned deeply to sin. He gave his life to sin. Finally God gave up on Saul.

He was a big, strong, intelligent young man. You could see the top of his head as he walked through a crowd. He was handsome and smart. But this man was too smart for his own good. He thought he didn't need God anymore.

Then one day God let him go, and his mind snapped. And Saul said to a young friend of his, "Stand...upon me and slay me: for anguish is come upon me" (II Samuel 1:9).

That's also what happened to Judas. He fooled around with sin. He tried it. Then he tried it again. He was young. He was strong. He thought he could get away with it. But one night the devil got ahold of him and wouldn't let go. And his mind snapped too. He went out and put a rope around his neck – he hanged himself from the limb of a tree. As he was writhing there, hanging by the neck, the limb broke and his body fell a long way down a cliff – and his stomach broke open and his bowels gushed out and he died. He waited too long. He fooled around with sin too long. And he "flipped out" and killed himself and went to Hell. He is called "the son of perdition," the son of Hell (John 17:12).

> "How shall we escape, if we neglect so great salvation?" (Hebrews 2:3).

Do not neglect Christ. Do not neglect salvation. You need to come to Jesus Christ. You need to have your sins washed away by His Blood. You need to be in a Bible-believing church on Sunday – and you need to be in church *every* Sunday. That's the way to escape from a lonely and meaningless life of sin.

CHAPTER TEN

MAN IN THREE STATES:
NATURAL, AWAKENED AND CONVERTED

The next two chapters are titled:

1. Man in Three States: Natural, Awakened and
    Converted.
2. The Location of the Risen Christ.

These chapters should be read slowly and prayerfully. They will help
you experience real conversion, so you will not be left behind.

The Righteous Servant

> "By his knowledge shall my righteous servant justify
> many; for he shall bear their iniquities" (Isaiah 53:11).

The fact that this speaks of Jesus is made clear in verse five:

> "But he was wounded for our transgressions, he was
> bruised for our iniquities: the chastisement of our peace
> was upon him; and with his stripes we are healed"
> (Isaiah 53:5).

The "righteous servant" in Isaiah 53 refers to Jesus, the Saviour
of mankind. He was sent by God the Father to die in your place, to
bear your sins, to pay the penalty for your transgressions.

But how do you receive the benefits of Christ's death? Isaiah
53:11 says, "By his knowledge." This means, in modern English,
"By the knowledge of him." Matthew Henry says it means by "faith
in him" (*Matthew Henry's Commentary on the Whole Bible,*
comment on Isaiah 53:11). You must have saving faith in Christ to
be converted. You must have a personal knowledge of Christ
Himself to be justified, to be counted as just and righteous in the

sight of God. Christ's righteousness is imputed to the sinner. The person who puts his faith in Him is clothed in His righteousness and escapes from judgment and Hell because Jesus, the "righteous servant," has justified him.

But notice that the passage says, "By his knowledge shall my righteous servant justify *many*." He will not save everyone. He will justify "many," but not *all*. The great majority of people will *never* experience salvation through Christ because they will refuse to go through conversion. You see, it takes a real conversion for a person to have a saving "knowledge" of Jesus Christ. And it is only "by his knowledge" that salvation comes to a lost person.

> "Except ye be converted...ye shall not enter into the kingdom of heaven" (Matthew 18:3).

You cannot have a true "knowledge" of Christ without being converted. You cannot be "saved" without being converted. You cannot be justified without being converted, and you cannot be raptured either!

Notice the end of Isaiah 53:11, "...for he shall bear their iniquities." The Hebrew meaning of "iniquities" is "perversities, mischief, sin" (*Strong's Concordance*). The wickedness that comes from your perverted and depraved heart must be forgiven by Jesus. "He shall bear their iniquities" (Isaiah 53:11). That's why Jesus was crucified. He allowed Himself to be killed so He could take the punishment for your sins. He was literally punished in your place, for your sins, on that Cross! You cannot be raptured (or get to Heaven at all) without having your sins paid for by Jesus Christ,

> "Who his own self bare our sins in his own body on the tree (the cross)..." (I Peter 2:24).

But you cannot receive the benefit of Christ's death unless you are converted. It is therefore *extremely* important for you to know about this subject:

> "Except ye be converted...ye shall not enter into the kingdom of heaven" (Matthew 18:3).

A person goes through three conditions, or states, when experiencing conversion.

> 1. A natural state
> 2. An awakened state
> 3. A converted state

For many, these states last a long time. For some, each condition is shorter. A few people move through these states in a matter of minutes. Let us examine them in detail.

Man in his Natural State

In I Corinthians 2:14 we read:

> "But the ***natural man*** receiveth not the things of the Spirit of God: for they are foolishness unto him: neither can he know them, because they are spiritually discerned" (I Corinthians 2:14).

That's your condition if you haven't experienced inward conversion. You are called a "natural man" or woman because that is the ***natural*** state of every person. We are born in this situation. We are "by nature the children of wrath" (Ephesians 2:3). Everyone who has not experienced inward conversion is in a "natural state."

Now, in the natural state, you despise, reject and hide your face from Jesus Christ, the Son of God. In Isaiah 53:3 we read:

> "He is despised and rejected of men...and we hid as it were our faces from him" (Isaiah 53:3).

Every unconverted person is described in this verse. ***Every one hides his face from Jesus, although most people don't have the self-awareness to realize it.***

Furthermore, in a natural state you turn to your own way:

> "All we like sheep have gone astray; we have turned every one to his own way" (Isaiah 53:6).

79

Like a sheep, you wander in your "own way." You go "astray" from Christ.

Consider six different ways people "go astray" in a natural state.

1. Those who are atheists have gone astray. The Bible tells us, "The fool hath said in his heart, There is no God" (Psalm 53:1). So, the Bible calls atheists "fools." Why are you an atheist, if that is your condition? The rest of the verse tells us, "Corrupt are they, and have done abominable iniquity: there is none that doeth good" (Psalm 53:1). The atheist does not believe in God because he is sinful and loves living a sinful life. He loves sinning so much that he rejects the idea of God. Psychiatrists call this emotional response "denial." If you are an atheist it is because you are in a state of "denial." *You deny the existence of God because you enjoy living a life of sin too much to seriously consider Jesus Christ.* If you are an atheist, you have gone astray in a life of sin and psychological "denial."

2. Those who reject the deity of Christ have gone astray as well. "All we like sheep have gone astray; we have turned every one to his own way" (Isaiah 53:6). Such people reject the fact that God became a man in the person of Jesus Christ. That's why they deny the atonement, the Blood sacrifice of Christ as a payment for sin. If you don't believe in the deity of Christ, the crucifixion seems like the death of a poor, confused zealot, rather than atonement for sin accomplished by God the Son. Although Christ bore "their iniquities" (Isaiah 53:11), *people who reject the deity of Christ do not see their need for His Blood to wash their sins away* (I John 1:7). If *you* don't think you need to have your sins washed away in His Blood, you have "gone astray."

3. Those who think like many Eastern people have gone astray also. People whose minds work this

way want to have "good luck" and "blessings." They never think in terms of sin and forgiveness. They are interested only in a happy and prosperous life. They never think about having their sins forgiven. They are like the fool who only thought about material blessings. God said to the man who thought like that, "Thou fool, this night thy soul shall be required of thee" (Luke 12:20). *The person who is only interested in having "good luck" and many physical "blessings" is a fool because his sins are not forgiven, and he will go to Hell when he dies.* People who think this way have gone astray. They have turned "to their own way" (Isaiah 53:6).

4. People who believe in salvation by works have also gone astray. They feel that they will be saved by confessing their sins, going to communion, saying their prayers, and trying to be good. "Being ignorant of God's righteousness, and going about to establish their own righteousness, (they) have not submitted themselves unto the righteousness of God" (Romans 10:3). Those who think this way feel they can earn salvation by being as good as possible. *They reject "the gift of righteousness" which Christ imparts to those who are converted* (cf. Romans 5:17). Instead of seeing salvation as a *gift,* they think they can *earn* it. One young man recently told me that he thinks he is saved because he changed his way of living. This view does not take into account the deep, inner sins of the mind and heart. Thinking like this will not save you from inward sins or past sins. You must have the Blood of Christ wash your sins away (I John 1:7). "It is the blood that maketh an atonement for the soul" (Leviticus 17:11). People who believe in salvation by their own efforts have gone astray. They "have turned every one to his own way" (Isaiah 53:6).

5. Emotional people have gone astray in their own way. "Great signs and wonders" have "deceived"

them (Matthew 24:24). ***They think that the Holy Spirit's work is to give them "good feelings," when the exact opposite is true!*** "And when he is come, he will reprove (convince) the world of sin" (John 16:8). The true purpose of the Holy Spirit is to make you feel sinful. Emotional people often think the Holy Spirit's work is to make them feel ***good!*** They stumble and go astray in their "own way" (Isaiah 53:6), because they reject conviction of sin, and therefore cannot be converted. In their refusal to come under deep conviction, they "have turned every one to his own way" (Isaiah 53:6).

6. Many evangelicals have gone astray as well. They have forgotten that salvation is a free gift (Ephesians 2:8-9). They think they are saved because they have learned the plan of salvation or have said a sinner's prayer, or made some other "decision." They will be shocked when they are sent to Hell at the Last Judgment (cf. Matthew 7:22-23). ***Those who think they can be saved by a mere human "decision" have gone astray.*** They too "have turned every one to his own way" (Isaiah 53:6).

Someone may say, "But Dr. Hymers, you've said that ***virtually everyone on earth is wrong!"*** Yes, you understood me! Read Isaiah 53:6 again:

"***All*** we like sheep have gone astray; we have turned ***every one*** to his own way..." (Isaiah 53:6).

The New Testament teaches this also:

"There is none righteous, no, not one: There is none that understandeth, there is none that seeketh after God" (Romans 3:10-11).

And notice how each one goes astray: they all do the same thing; every one of them hides their face from Jesus Christ. They do it in different ways, but they ***all*** do it!

> "He is despised and rejected of men...and we hid as it
> were our faces from him; he was despised, and we
> esteemed him not" (Isaiah 53:3).

Man in his natural and unconverted state rejects Jesus Christ.
You may *say* that you believe in Him, but your inner heart
actually rejects Him.

> "This people draweth nigh unto me with their mouth,
> and honoureth me with their lips: but their heart is far
> from me" (Matthew 15:8).

Man in an Awakened State

The second state is the condition of awakening. You wake up
from the false ideas you had while you were in a natural state. The
Bible says:

> "*Awake thou that sleepest,* and arise from the dead, and
> Christ shall give thee light" (Ephesians 5:14).

You wake up to the thought of dying without Christ. People
who were once content with their lives wake up to the certainty of
their own death. They wake up to the fact that they are *not ready* to
die. Are *you* ready to die? Are you ready to face God Almighty?
Have you been awakened to the fact that death is coming *very soon
for you?* Serious thoughts about eternity will fill your mind when
you are awakened.
*You will also be awakened to the awfulness of the sins you
have committed.* You will think of some great sin you once did.
You will be horrified by it. You will think about the fact that God
knows all about that sin, and has it recorded in His books in Heaven
(cf. Revelation 20:12-15). You will be disgusted and ashamed of
your own sin when you are awakened.
*You will also think about your inward sinfulness when you are
awakened.* This thought will also come into your mind: "My heart is
very sinful and very far from God." You will be horrified by your
sinful thoughts, your inward lack of love for God, and the deadness
of your prayers. The cold lifelessness of your heart toward God will

trouble you deeply when you are awakened. You will realize that a person with a sinful heart like yours has no hope. You will see how wicked and guilty you are in the sight of a holy God. You will see that there is no way for you to escape His wrath and judgment. You will understand that you *deserve* to be punished by God when you begin to be awakened! You will then say with John Newton, the author of "Amazing Grace":

> O Lord, how vile am I,
> Unholy and unclean!
> How can I dare to venture nigh
> With such a load of sin?
>
> Is this polluted heart
> A dwelling place for Thee?
> Swarming, alas! in every part,
> What evils do I see!
> ("O Lord, How Vile am I" by John Newton, 1725-1807)

There can be no awakening without a sharp sense of sin and self-condemnation. There can be no real conversion without a sense of inner filthiness.

The State of Conversion

When a man or woman is converted, they are in the last of the three states. At first, they were natural men and women. They made excuses for rejecting Christ, or they pretended to accept Him while they really did not. They lived their lives in security, never fearing Hell or condemnation for their sin. They were asleep in sin. They comforted themselves by thinking they were no worse than others. They thought they were saved. Actually they were "dead in trespasses and sins" (Ephesians 2:1). But they did not know it. They were happy with themselves.

That's the way *you* are, isn't it? You think you're saved. You deceive yourself. You *trick* yourself into thinking that you are O.K., because you are in a natural state.

When you are awakened, you will then be horror-stricken by how blind you were! You will then realize how evil your sins are. You won't know how to get rid of your sins. You will be desperate.

84

Then, at long last, some of you will submit to Jesus Christ, and rest in Him. Your mind will be occupied with the thought of Jesus dying to pay for your sins on the Cross. You will be filled with the thought of Him rising from the dead and ascending into Heaven, to the right hand of God. Your thoughts will go out to Christ in Heaven. You will be washed from your sins by His Blood. You will then be converted.

> Guilty, vile and helpless we;
>> Spotless Lamb of God was He;
> "Full atonement" can it be?
>> Hallelujah! What a Saviour!
>>> ("Hallelujah, What a Saviour!" by Philip P. Bliss, 1838-1876).

CHAPTER ELEVEN

THE LOCATION OF THE RISEN CHRIST

"Where is he?" (John 7:11).

It is very important for you to know *where* Jesus is today. If you didn't know where He was at the time of your supposed conversion, I truly doubt that you're saved. How could you have come to Him without knowing where He is? If this thought gives you an "uncomfortable feeling," think how much more uncomfortable you will feel when you are left behind at the rapture! I urge you to read what I have written in this chapter slowly and with great seriousness.

Where Is Jesus?

When Jesus went to Jerusalem for the last time, certain Jews were looking for Him. They said, "Where is he?" (John 7:11). Many thousands of people today are as lost and confused as they were. "Where is he?" They have no idea where Jesus is. They call themselves Christians, yet they don't have any more knowledge of where Jesus is than those people in Jerusalem long ago.

In Hebrews 8:1 we are told exactly where He is today,

> "We have such an high priest, who is set on the right hand of the throne of the Majesty in the heavens; A minister of the sanctuary, and of the true tabernacle, which the Lord pitched, and not man" (Hebrews 8:1-2).

Dr. J. Vernon McGee gave this comment:

> Christ did something which no priest in the Old Testament ever did. There is not a priest in the line of Aaron who ever had a chair in the tabernacle where he sat down. He was on the run all the time. Why? Because he had work to do. All these things are shadows that point to a finished sacrifice. Now that

> Christ has died, all has been fulfilled...*He sat down*
> *because He had finished our redemption.* (J. Vernon
> McGee, *Thru the Bible*, volume V, p. 557).

And Hebrews 8:1 tells us the exact place where Christ sat down when
He ascended into Heaven: "On the right hand of the throne of the
Majesty in the heavens" (Hebrews 8:1b).

Another verse in the book of Hebrews tells us,

> "This man, after he had offered one sacrifice for sins for
> ever, sat down on the right hand of God" (Hebrews
> 10:12).

This verse corrects the idea that Christ is offered up as a sacrifice in
each communion service. It says, "After he had offered *one sacrifice*
for sins for ever." Jesus' sacrifice on the Cross was done once "for
ever." When Jesus died He said, "It is finished" (John 19:30). He
paid the penalty for all of your sins *once,* on the Cross. There is no
need for a new sacrifice. The moment that you truly believe in Jesus,
His payment for sins on the Cross becomes yours, and all of your sins
are eternally paid for and blotted out of God's records. "It is
finished."

Then Hebrews 10:12 continues:

> "After he had offered one sacrifice for sins for ever, sat
> down on the right hand of God" (Hebrews 10:12).

Jesus sat down at the right side of God, up in Heaven, in another
dimension. That's where He is right now!

Let us consider three things about this great doctrine:

1. Where Jesus sat down
2. When Jesus sat down
3. Why Jesus sat down

Where Jesus Sat Down

We have already seen that He sat down at God's right hand in
Heaven. Jesus told us He would do that even before He was
crucified:

> "Hereafter shall the Son of man *sit on the right hand of the power of God.* Then said they all, Art thou then the Son of God? And he said unto them, Ye say that I am. And they said, What need we any further witness? for we ourselves have heard of his own mouth" (Luke 22:69-71).

Matthew records these additional words:

> "Jesus saith unto him (the high priest), Thou hast said: nevertheless I say unto you, *Hereafter shall ye see the Son of man sitting on the right hand of power,* and coming in the clouds of heaven. Then the high priest rent (or tore) his clothes, saying, He hath spoken blasphemy; what further need have we of witnesses? behold, now ye have heard his blasphemy. What think ye? They answered and said, He is guilty of death. Then did they spit in his face, and buffeted him (i.e. beat Him); and others smote (hit) him with the palms of their hands, Saying, Prophesy unto us, thou Christ, Who is he that smote thee?" (Matthew 26:64-68).

They spit on Jesus and beat Him for saying that He would sit "on the right hand of power" (Matthew 26:64).

Oh, how clear are these words that Jesus gave the night before He was crucified! How plainly He said that He would "sit on the right hand of the power of God"! (Luke 22:69).

Then, the New Testament tells us the same thing repeatedly. In Mark 16:19, we read:

> "So then after the Lord had spoken unto them, he was received up into heaven, and sat down on the right hand of God" (Mark 16:19).

In his sermon at Pentecost, Peter said:

> "This Jesus hath God raised up, whereof we all are witnesses. Therefore *being by the right hand of God exalted,* and having received of the Father the promise of the Holy Ghost, he hath shed forth this, which ye

now see and hear. For David is not ascended into the heavens: but he saith himself, *The Lord said unto my Lord, Sit thou on my right hand,* Until I make thy foes thy footstool" (Acts 2:32-35).

In that same sermon, Peter quoted from Psalm 110:1,

"The Lord said unto my Lord, *Sit thou at my right hand,* until I make thine enemies thy footstool" (Psalm 110:1).

This prophetic verse in the Old Testament showed in advance that Jesus would sit down at the right hand of God in Heaven.

In another sermon Peter said:

"The God of our fathers raised up Jesus, whom ye slew and hanged on a tree. *Him hath God exalted with his right hand* to be a Prince and a Saviour..."
(Acts 5:30-31).

Stephen's great sermon before the Sanhedrin ended with them stoning him to death as he cried out:

"Behold, I see the heavens opened, and *the Son of man standing on the right hand of God"* (Acts 7:56).

Dr. J. Vernon McGee gave this touching comment:

Stephen goes into the presence of Christ who is standing to meet him. Stephen is the first martyr of the church to go to be with his Lord. (J. Vernon McGee, *Thru the Bible,* volume IV, p. 541).

Stephen's words made a deep impression on the unconverted Paul, who heard him say, "I see the heavens opened, and the Son of man standing on the right hand of God" (Acts 7:56). Paul was nearby and heard him say this (cf. Acts 7:58). The words of this dying man had a great impact on Paul. Dr. McGee says:

Stephen was a tremendous witness to Saul (later named Paul). Stephen was the one, I believe, who prepared Saul for the appearance of the Lord Jesus on the

Damascus road. (J. Vernon McGee, *Thru the Bible*, ibid.)

This message of Stephen's was burned forever into Paul's soul. Later, after he was converted, Paul wrote:

> "Who is he that condemneth? It is Christ that died, yea, rather, that is risen again, *who is even at the right hand of God,* who also maketh intercession for us" (Romans 8:34).

Again, Paul wrote,

> "According to the working of his (God's) mighty power, Which he wrought in Christ, when he raised him from the dead, and *set him at his own right hand* in the heavenly places" (Ephesians 1:19-20).

Again, in the Epistle to the Colossians, Paul said:

> "If ye then be risen with Christ, seek those things which are above, where *Christ sitteth on the right hand of God.* Set your affection on things above, not on things on the earth" (Colossians 3:1-2).

In Hebrews 12:2, he wrote:

> "Looking unto Jesus the author and finisher of our faith; who for the joy that was set before him endured the cross, despising the shame, and *is set down at the right hand of the throne of God"* (Hebrews 12:2).

Earlier in this Epistle, he said that Christ "sat down on the right hand of the Majesty on high" (Hebrews 1:3). He also said, "We have such an high priest, who is set on the right hand of the throne of the Majesty in the heavens" (Hebrews 8:1). Again, he said, "But this man, after he had offered one sacrifice for sins for ever, sat down on the right hand of God" (Hebrews 10:12).

Peter also wrote about this subject in his first epistle:

"Jesus Christ: Who is gone into heaven, and *is on the right hand of God;* angels and authorities and powers being made subject unto him" (I Peter 3:22).

I have given you many of the statements in the Bible, both in the Old and New Testaments, which show beyond any shadow of a doubt that Jesus Christ is now seated at the right side of Almighty God in Heaven.

Yet, when a pastor asks questions of those who come for counselling after his sermons, he will often discover that people don't know where Jesus is. *Can we blame lost people who come to visit church a few times for not knowing where the Saviour is if they are not told?*

A Deadly Error

A Sunday School teacher once said to me, "Christ is in the air all around us." That is a common misconception today. I think it infiltrates our churches indirectly from the New Age movement. *But it is a deadly error.* A person may know the plan of salvation, and be in church every Sunday, but if he is as ignorant of the location of Christ as that Sunday School teacher, he is still lost. How about *you?* If you think Jesus is in the air all around you, I believe you are still lost.

I don't care who you are, or what position you hold in your church. No one can be saved without believing in Jesus. And no one can truly believe in Jesus unless he knows where Jesus is. That's why the Bible repeatedly, in verse after verse, in chapter after chapter, in the Psalms, in Matthew, in Mark, in Luke, in Acts, in Romans, in Ephesians, in Colossians, in Hebrews, in I Peter, and in many other books of the Bible, tells us where Jesus is located right now.

God would not have put so many verses in the Bible if He didn't think it was highly important for you to know where Christ is located today.

If you don't know where He is, you are as lost as those Jews who said, "Where is he?" (John 7:11). People cannot come to Jesus unless they know where He is, because He said:

91

> "Come unto me, all ye that labour and are heavy laden,
> and I will give you rest" (Matthew 11:28).

And no one can come to Jesus unless he knows that Christ is in Heaven, at God's right hand.

I belabor this point because many pastors will read this book. To them I say, "Preacher, if you don't *ask* lost people where they think Jesus is, you will not be able to correct them! You must give them the Bible answer. Many lost people say that Jesus is in their hearts. But He isn't. If the lost believe and trust a Jesus in their own deceitful hearts they will go to Hell, because He is not there!

I asked one girl, "Where is Jesus right now?" She wrongly said, "He's in my heart." I said, "How big is He?" She replied, "He's about a half inch high, and He walked through a little door that was made in a hole in the side of my heart." She learned this absurd nonsense in Sunday School. She should have been told where Jesus *really* is – in Heaven, at the right hand of God.

You can't come to Jesus if you don't know where He is. And this is not an unimportant issue, or a side issue, at all! It is at the very heart of the gospel, repeated over and over, throughout the Bible. If the resurrection and ascension of Christ aren't central parts of the gospel, what is?

Preacher, you must ask your people where they think Jesus is, or they will go to Hell. They cannot believe in Him, trust Him, and come to Him if they don't know where He is! *Thousands of people in our churches are lost because they were told to come to Jesus and believe in Him without being told where He is!* This happens because preachers don't explain the resurrection and ascension of Christ often enough. I find that I must mention these Bible doctrines in virtually every sermon!

Romans 10:9 and I Corinthians 15:17 show the centrality of the resurrection of Christ. This should be proclaimed in all of our evangelistic sermons, along with His ascension and mediatorial work in Heaven. The main reason so many people are confused on this important subject is because preachers don't ask simple questions like this: "Where is Jesus right now?" *Preacher, you have to know what they think! You can only find out by asking questions!* Even if you preach on this subject and explain it, many will not hear what you are saying. Only by questioning those who respond after the sermon can you find out whether they "got it." That's why preachers need a quiet place where they can ask questions and *listen* to the answers after they preach.

When Did This Happen?

First, Christ sat down at God's right hand *after He purged our sins on the Cross.* That means He sat down after He was crucified and resurrected.

> "When he had by himself purged our sins, sat down on the right hand of the Majesty on high" (Hebrews 1:3b).

Second, He sat down at God's right hand after He offered His Blood in Heaven:

> "For every high priest is ordained to offer gifts and sacrifices: wherefore it is of necessity that this man (Jesus) have somewhat also to offer" (Hebrews 8:3).

> "But into the second (the Holy of Holies in the tabernacle) went the high priest alone once every year, not without blood, which he offered for...the errors of the people" (Hebrews 9:7).

> "Neither by the blood of goats and calves, but by his own blood he entered in once into the holy place (the Holy of Holies in Heaven), having obtained eternal redemption for us" (Hebrews 9:12).

Dr. J. Vernon McGee commented:

> I believe this verse proves that Christ took His blood literally to Heaven. *If that is not what the writer is talking about here, I do not know what he is saying.* (J. Vernon McGee, *Thru the Bible*, volume V, p. 566).

Dr. Rod Bell, president of the Fundamental Baptist Fellowship, made this statement in a recent editorial in *Frontline* Magazine titled, "The Precious Blood of Christ,"

With good reason, then, is the Lord Jesus Christ called the "lamb without blemish and without spot" (I Pet. 1:19). His blood was untainted with Adam's sin. No guilt or corruption was transmitted to Him, in stark contrast to every other person ever born.

Therefore, His blood is incorruptible, emphasizing its purity. But as we shall now see, "incorruptible blood" emphasizes much more than that. *Not only was it precious blood, but it is indestructible blood. Clearly, Christ's blood was incapable of corrupting or decaying.* What does this mean?

The meaning of "incorruptible" is clearly inferred by the reference to Christ's body not seeing corruption. In Psalm 16:10 we have a prophecy which was fulfilled in the resurrection of Christ. "For thou wilt not leave my soul in hell; neither wilt thou suffer thine Holy One to see corruption." This text was quoted by Peter on the day of Pentecost in Acts 2:27, 31. He told his audience that David had not spoken of himself.

Which leaves us with a question. *Where is the blood of Christ today? Has it been destroyed? Has it been corrupted? Has it been soaked up in the sand? Many would like you to believe that the answer to these questions is "yes." The scholars would like to explain it away. But the Word of God says otherwise. It has been raised to heaven. That is the simple answer, the only answer warranted by this infallible Book, our authoritative voice of faith and practice.*

Dr. Bell is right! Amen! Amen! And Amen!

Christ sat down after He presented His precious Blood in the Holy of Holies in Heaven. "He entered into the holy place" (Hebrews 9:12) and put His Blood on the heavenly Ark of the Covenant. The Bible says that our high priest went in "not without blood" (Hebrews 9:7; cf. 9:11, 24). Dr. McGee said:

> I say to you very definitely and dogmatically that *I believe His Blood is even now in Heaven,* and throughout endless ages it will be there to remind us of the awful price Christ paid to redeem us. (J. Vernon McGee, *Thru the Bible*, volume V, p. 560).

94

In the 19th century C. H. Spurgeon said:

> *I know that his precious blood in heaven prevails with God on behalf of them that come unto him:* And since I come unto Him, I know by faith that I have an interest in his perpetual intercession. (C. H. Spurgeon, "The Warrant of Faith," *Metropolitan Tabernacle Pulpit*, volume 9, p. 530).

In the fifth century A.D. Chrysostom said:

> His Blood was borne up into Heaven...carried into the Holy place (*Homilies on Hebrews*, Homily XXXIII, in *A Select Library of the Nicene and Post-Nicene Fathers of the Christian Church*, Grand Rapids: Eerdmans, 1978 reprint, volume XIV, p. 517).

The *Scofield Study Bible* said the same thing 1,400 years later:

> The high priest entering the holiest, typifies Christ entering "heaven itself" with "His own blood" for us (note on Leviticus 16:5).

And in the 18th century, Charles Wesley wrote,

> His Blood atoned for all our race
> And sprinkles *now* the throne of grace,
> And sprinkles *now* the throne of grace.
> ("Arise! My Soul, Arise!" by Charles Wesley, 1707-1788).

Christian leaders across the ages have been in agreement with the Bible that the Blood of Christ is now in Heaven. Christ sat down at the right hand of God after He had placed His incorruptible Blood on the mercy seat, in the Holy of Holies, in Heaven. *"The blood of sprinkling" is listed in the Bible as one of the things in Heaven (Hebrews 12:22-24).*

Why Jesus Sat Down

Christ sat down for a highly important reason – to pray for you. In Hebrews 7:25 we are told:

"Wherefore he is able also to save them to the uttermost
(i.e. forever) that come unto God by him, seeing he
ever liveth to make intercession (to pray) for them"
(Hebrews 7:25).

Often I have nearly quit the Christian life, or nearly stumbled. I
am greatly surprised to find myself in the ministry after forty-three
years. There have been so many pitfalls, so many battles, so many
discouragements, so many personal weaknesses, so many doubts,
fears, disappointments, and so little faith on my part. I often find
myself saying with Paul, "Who is sufficient for these things?" (II
Corinthians 2:16). I am really *quite* surprised that I am still in the
ministry after forty-three years! How have I been able to go on all
this time? Not by my own strength or power, I can assure you!

But I have a Saviour who's praying for me in Heaven. And His
prayers are effectual. When Jesus prays for this weak, bald-headed,
stoop-shouldered, discouraged little inner-city preacher, again and
again God answers the prayers of His Son for me. I am saved
because "he ever liveth to make intercession for (me)" (Hebrews
7:25).

I have heard good men say, "The key to the Christian life is your
prayers." There is a great deal of truth to that. But I'd rather say,
"The __main__ key to the Christian life is __Jesus'__ prayers for you!"

He ever lives above, for me to intercede;
His all-redeeming love, His precious blood to plead...

The Father hears Him pray, His dear anointed One;
He cannot turn away The presence of His Son.
("Arise! My Soul, Arise!" by Charles Wesley, 1707-1788).

Never forget *where* Jesus is – at God's right hand in Heaven.
Never forget *why* He is there. He presented His Blood to God to
cleanse your sins. Never forget that He sits hour after hour praying
for you. *With Jesus praying for you, how can you fail?* The whole
secret of the Christian life is this: His Blood cleanses you from sin,
and He is praying for you!

And yes, He is praying for you too, sinner. He is praying for you to trust Him, believe in Him, and let Him save you. Jesus Christ is praying for you to get saved.

> I have a Saviour, He's pleading in glory,
> A dear, loving Saviour, though earth friends be few;
> And now He is watching in tenderness o'er me,
> But oh, that my Saviour were your Saviour too!
> For you He is praying, for you He is praying,
> For you He is praying, He's praying for you.
>> ("I Am Praying For You" by S. O'Malley Clough, 1837-1910,
>> chorus altered by R. L. Hymers, Jr.)

CHAPTER TWELVE

YOUR CONVERSION

"Except ye be converted, and become as little children,
ye shall not enter into the kingdom of heaven"
(Matthew 18:3).

If what I've written so far has made you think you may not be ready for the rapture, I hope that you will read this chapter carefully. You should read it several times and think about it very deeply as you do.

What Are You Trusting?

You already have an opinion about salvation. Everyone does. You must be ready to throw away your present opinion about how to be saved if you want the real thing. If you had a false conversion, it is because you trusted something other than Jesus Christ. As you read the following list try to see which category fits you best, so you can change your thinking.

1. People with a liturgical background often trust their own good works to save them rather than the Son of God. *They think they are saved because they go to religious services, try to follow Jesus, confess their sins, obey the Ten Commandments, or follow the "Golden Rule."* But no one experiences salvation by being religious or trying to be good. The Bible says:

   > "Not by works of righteousness which we have done, but according to his mercy he saved us..." (Titus 3:5).

   True salvation only comes by trusting Christ, in a converting, one-time act of faith. Every person whose conversion is recorded in the Bible was saved through such an act of faith in Christ. Jesus is not angry with you. He loves you. You can turn to Him and believe in Him now. He is the Son of God, seated at God the Father's right hand in Heaven. You can throw yourself on Jesus and His Blood will wash away your sins. The instant you do that, you are saved. You can go directly to Jesus and trust Him. He will save you now.

2.   People with evangelical backgrounds often trust the fact that they have "gone forward," said the "sinner's prayer," "asked Jesus to come into their heart," or the fact that they believe "the plan of salvation." *They trust a "decision" they once made rather than the Son of God.* This is really salvation by works also. None of these "works" will save you.

> "For by grace are ye saved through faith...Not of works, lest any man should boast" (Ephesians 2:8-9).

You must give up the human "decision" you made and trust Jesus Christ Himself. He is alive right now in Heaven, seated beside God the Father. You can go directly to Jesus and He will cleanse your sins with His Blood. But it must be a new and living trust in Jesus. Give up your old "decision" and come now to the Son of God Himself.

3.   People with charismatic backgrounds often trust feelings or experiences rather than the Son of God. *They often think they are saved because they have "received" the Holy Spirit, or feel peace and blessings in their lives. They trust these feelings and experiences rather than the Son of God.* These people often seek "assurance"

when in fact they have never been converted in the first place.

If you hope to get to Heaven by "being good," you are still lost. If you hope to get to Heaven by saying a "sinner's prayer" or "coming forward" or believing "the plan of salvation," you are still lost. If you are relying on a "feeling" you once had to get you to Heaven, you are still lost. *You are trusting something you, yourself have experienced or accomplished.* *You have not fully trusted Jesus, the Son of God.*

Your Greatest Sin

The greatest sin you have committed is rejecting Jesus Christ. You may not admit it to yourself, but that is what you have really done.

> "He is despised and rejected of men...and we hid as it were our faces from him; he was despised, and we esteemed him not" (Isaiah 53:3).

The word "gospel" means "good news." The good news tells you that Jesus died on the Cross to pay for your sins. He is now alive in Heaven, at the right hand of God. The good news is given to you in these words:

> "Christ died for our sins according to the Scriptures; And that he was buried, and that he rose again the third day according to the Scriptures" (I Corinthians 15:3-4).

Notice that the passage says, "Christ died for our *sins*."

The reason Jesus died was to pay the penalty for your *sins*. The Bible says:

> "The Lord hath laid on him (Jesus) the *iniquity (or sin)* of us all" (Isaiah 53:6).

> "For Christ also hath once suffered for *sins*, the just (Jesus) for the unjust (you), that he might bring us to God..." (I Peter 3:18).

100

> "But this man (Jesus), after he had offered one sacrifice
> *for sins* for ever, sat down on the right hand of God"
> (Hebrews 10:12).

All of us went "astray" before we were converted (Isaiah 53:6). We had false ideas about how to be saved, such as the ones I have mentioned. Our greatest sin was that we rejected Jesus, the only one who could save us from *the guilt of sin, and punishment for our sins.*

That is why God sent the Holy Spirit to reprove (or convince) us of our *sin* (John 16:8). "Of *sin*, because they believe not on me," Jesus said (John 16:9). You have many *sins* that need to be cleansed by the Blood of Jesus. But your greatest *sin* is that you have relied on something else to save you from *sin* other than Jesus Himself.

The reason Jesus came to earth was to save you from the guilt of *sin.* The Bible says:

> "Thou shalt call his name JESUS: *for he shall save his
> people from their <u>sins</u>"* (Matthew 1:21).

The very name of Jesus shows His main purpose for coming to this earth: to "save his people from their sins." The name "Jesus" means "Jehovah saves." Jehovah is the name of God. The first part of Jesus' name (Je) is short for the name of God. The second part of His name (sus) indicates that God saves us from sin – through *Jesus*, and *only* through Jesus.

> "Neither is there salvation in any other: for there is none
> other name under heaven given among men, whereby
> we must be saved" (Acts 4:12).

Your greatest sin is replacing Jesus with a good work, feeling, "decision" or doctrine.

The "Faith" of a Demon

Oh, I know, you probably have some sort of "belief" in Jesus. But it is probably only a doctrinal belief. You believe things *about*

Him, but you have not put your trust *in Him*. Your "faith" in Jesus is no better than the "faith" of a demon.

When Jesus went into the synagogue at Capernaum, one demon cried out, "I know thee who thou art; the Holy One of God" (Luke 4:34). Later in the day, when the sun was setting, many demon possessed people came where Jesus was. These demons screamed, "Thou art Christ the Son of God" (Luke 4:41a). The verse ends by saying, "They knew that he was Christ" (Luke 4:41b). *So, if you believe Christ is the Saviour sent from God, your "faith" is no better than that of a demon.* This "faith" will not save you from sin, or from Hell, the eternal punishment of sin. One day Jesus will say to you,

> "Depart from me, ye cursed, into everlasting fire,
> prepared for the devil and his angels" (Matthew 25:41).

Those demons who knew that He was the Saviour, and said so, will be in Hell according to Matthew 25:41. They are the Devil's "angels." You will also be in Hell if your "faith" in Jesus goes no farther than that of a demon.

I heard a preacher give a brilliant sermon on Luke 18:9-14 the other night. He exposed virtually all forms of decisional salvation, showing that coming forward, saying the sinner's prayer, going to church, etc., cannot save you. Then he said you have to believe in Jesus. "Perfect," I thought. But *then* he said, "Believing in Jesus means that you believe He died to pay for your sins." I thought, "Oh, no! He confuses believing this *fact* with believing *in Jesus, Himself!*" You have to look to the Son of God in Heaven to be saved. Otherwise your faith goes no farther than that of a demon.

Believe "Into" and "On" Jesus

In John 3:18 we read these words:

> "He that believeth *on* him (Jesus) is not condemned..."
> (John 3:18).

Notice that the King James judiciously uses the English word "on." "He that believeth *on* him is not condemned." The word translated "on" is "eis." According to Dr. Zodhiates, it means "the primary idea of motion into a place or thing." Your faith must go *into* Jesus – up in Heaven at the right hand of God.

> "Seek those things which are above, where Christ sitteth on the right hand of God. Set your affection on things above..." (Colossians 3:1-2).

So you must believe "into" Jesus, up in Heaven.

Then, the Bible says:

> "Believe *on* the Lord Jesus Christ, and thou shalt be saved..." (Acts 16:31).

The word translated "on" in this verse is a different Greek word, the word "epi." It means "upon" according to *Strong's Concordance*. The idea here is that you throw yourself *upon* Jesus. Literally "Believe *upon* the Lord Jesus Christ, and thou shalt be saved" (Acts 16:31).

If you want to have your sins forgiven, all of them – forever – believe "into" Jesus up in Heaven. And believe "upon" Him. *Throw yourself on Him as a man throws himself out of the window of a burning building "into" and "upon" the net that firemen have spread below to catch him as he falls. Throw yourself "into" and "upon" Jesus Christ!*

> "Believe *on* the Lord Jesus Christ, and thou shalt be saved..." (Acts 16:31).

No Prayer Needed

There is no need to confess your sins. Confession will only confuse you. Simply believe *on* Jesus! Do not say any prayer at all. Simply believe *on* Jesus! Do not *ask* Jesus to save you or forgive your sins. Simply believe *on* Him!

> The moment a sinner believes,
> And trusts in his crucified God,
> His pardon at once he receives,
> Redemption in full through His blood.
>   ("The Moment a Sinner Believes" by Joseph Hart, 1712-1768).

"The moment a sinner believes (in Jesus)...His pardon at once he receives." The very second that you throw yourself on and into Jesus all of your sins – past, present and future – are washed away everlastingly in His Blood. Then you will be able to say,

> "Unto him that loved us, and washed us from our sins in his own blood" (Revelation 1:5).

> "The blood of Jesus Christ his Son cleanseth us from all sin" (I John 1:7).

Why not believe on Jesus right now? Why not get down on your knees, without praying, and simply believe on Jesus? Do not ask Him to save you. ***Simply believe on the Son of God.*** Will you do that now?

Then, get into a Bible-believing church and attend every service. The New Testament knows nothing of a "churchless" Christianity.

> "And the Lord added to the church (at Jerusalem) daily such as should be saved" (Acts 2:47).

The person who is truly converted will be ready when Jesus comes!

> While its hosts cry Hosanna, from Heaven descending,
> With glorified saints and the angels attending
> With grace on His brow, like a halo of glory,
> Will Jesus receive "His own."
>
> Oh, joy! Oh, delight! should we go without dying,
> No sickness, no sadness, no dread and no crying,
> Caught up through the clouds with our Lord into glory,
> When Jesus receives "His own."
>
> O Lord Jesus, how long, how long Ere we shout the glad song,
> Christ returneth! Hallelujah! Hallelujah! Amen, Hallelujah! Amen.
> ("Christ Returneth" by H. L. Turner, 19th century)